Diversity in Family Formation

European Studies of Population

VOLUME 8

The book series *European Studies of Population (ESPO)* aims at disseminating population and family research, with special relevance for Europe. It may analyse past, present and/or future trends, as well as their determinants and consequences.
The character of the series is multidisciplinary, including formal demographic analyses, as well as social, economic and/or historical population and family studies.
The following types of studies are of primary importance: (a) internationally relevant studies, (b) European comparative studies, (c) innovative theoretical and methodological studies, and (d) policy-relevant scientific studies. The series may include monographs, edited volumes and reference works.
The book series is published under the auspices of the *European Associaiton for Population Studies (EAPS)*

Editorial Offices:

Gijs *Beets*
Netherlands Interdisciplinary
Demographic Institute (NIDI)
PO Box 11650
NL-2502 AR The Hague, Netherlands
Phone.: +31 70 356 5200
Fax.: +31 70 364 7187
E-mail: beets@nidi.nl

Fred *Deven*
Population and Family
Studies Centre (CBGS)
Markiesstraat 1
B-1000 Brussels, Belgium
Phone.: +32 2 553 3588
Fax: +32 2 553 3419
E-mail: cbgs@wvc.vlaanderen.be

Technical Editors:

Joan *Vrind*

Anita Wouters

The titles published in this series are listed at the end of this volume

Diversity in Family Formation

The 2nd Demographic Transition in Belgium and The Netherlands

edited by

JOOP DE BEER
Statistics Netherlands, Voorburg, The Netherlands

and

FRED DEVEN
CBGS, Brussels, Belgium

Contributors

Joop de Beer
Marc Callens
Martine Corijn
Fred Deven
Arie de Graaf
Wim van Hoorn
Andries de Jong
Edith Lodewijckx
Dorien Manting

KLUWER ACADEMIC PUBLISHERS
DORDRECHT / BOSTON / LONDON

A C.I.P. Catalogue record for this book is available from the Library of Congress.

ISBN 0-7923-6461-9

Published by Kluwer Academic Publishers,
P.O. Box 17, 3300 AA Dordrecht, The Netherlands.

Sold and distributed in North, Central and South America
by Kluwer Academic Publishers,
101 Philip Drive, Norwell, MA 02061, U.S.A.

In all other countries, sold and distributed
by Kluwer Academic Publishers,
P.O. Box 322, 3300 AH Dordrecht, The Netherlands.

Printed on acid-free paper

Printed in the Netherlands.

TABLE OF CONTENTS

PREFACE

During the last decades family formation behaviour has changed significantly in Western Europe. The increase in non-marital cohabitation and extra-marital fertility, the postponement of marriage and parenthood, and the increase in childlessness have lead to an increased variety of family forms. Even though similar trends have been observed across Europe, there are still remarkable differences between individual countries. Some demographers emphasise the similarity of developments in different countries by suggesting that there is one common Second Demographic Transition, similar to the First Demographic Transition which was observed in all developed countries some hundred years ago. Other demographers underline the diversity of demographic behaviour.

In addressing these issues the book by de Beer & Deven (eds.) presents an in-depth analysis of changes in family formation in two countries, viz. Belgium and the Netherlands, rather than giving a rough overview of demographic changes in many countries. Usually comparative studies focus on the differences between Northern and Southern Europe. Generally it is assumed that new trends begin in the north and subsequently spread to the south. A comparison of the Netherlands and Belgium is interesting because, on the one hand, these two countries to some extent can be regarded as representatives of Northern and Southern Europe respectively, while on the other hand these neighbouring countries are not that different that it is hardly feasible to interpret demographic differences because of an abundance of potential causes of these differences.

In order to interpret demographic differences across countries it is essential to have information about the interaction between family formation behaviour and the economic, institutional and cultural context. This requires an in-depth analysis of data-sets including both demographic and non-demographic variables. Data from population censuses, vital registrations and population registers do not provide sufficient information for this purpose. For this reason in the late1980s the Population Activities Unit (PAU) of the United Nations Economic Commission for Europe (ECE) initiated a research programme which aimed to conduct comparable fertility and family surveys in about twenty ECE member countries. Belgium and the Netherlands participated in this programme. In the 1990s the *Population and Family Study Centre CBGS* and *Statistics Netherlands* held fertility and family surveys that were consistent with the PAU recommendations. For Belgium a survey was conducted in 1991 in the Flemish region and in 1992 in the Brussels region. No data were collected for Wallonia. For the Netherlands a survey was held in 1993. The present volume presents the results of analyses of the data obtained from these surveys. The analyses were performed jointly by researchers from CBGS and the Department of population of Statistics Netherlands. The authors of each chapter are listed in alphabetical order.

Prof. dr. Thérèse JACOBS
General director, CBGS, *Population and Family Study Centre*, Brussels

Dr. Rolf VERHOEF
Head of Department Population, CBS, *Statistics Netherlands*, Voorburg

LIST OF TABLES

LIST OF FIGURES

1. GENERAL INTRODUCTION
A Bird's Eye view of Belgian and Dutch Fertility and Family Data

Joop de Beer and Fred Deven

1.1 Introduction

Since the 1960s fertility and family behaviour have changed drastically in Western-European countries. The changes include a decrease in the number of large families, an increase in childlessness and extra-marital childbearing, postponement of marriage and parenthood, and an increase in non-married cohabitation and in divorce. These developments are not isolated trends, but are closely associated with each other. Similar trends have been observed in many countries. However, despite many similarities, there are also important differences between countries. For example, in Southern European countries fertility rates have declined to much lower levels than in Northern Europe whereas marriage rates, by contrast, have fallen much more sharply in the latter.

The similar demographic developments in many European countries raise the question whether inter-country differences will ultimately disappear, i.e. whether there will be convergence between European countries in family and fertility behaviour. One may assume that different countries follow the same pattern of change and that differences between countries are due to differences in the timing of the onset and/or the speed of the process. Alternatively, one may assume that different countries follow other trajectories and that differences in fertility and family behaviour will persist.

J. de Beer and F. Deven (eds.), Diversity in Family Formation, 1–10.

In introducing the concept of the second demographic transition, Lesthaeghe and Van de Kaa (1986) suggest that different countries follow similar developments. Van de Kaa (1997) argues that differences between European countries can mainly be attributed to variations in the pace of change and that the basic pattern of change is similar across countries ("All countries go through the same sequence"). The changes in fertility and family behaviour can be explained by economic, technological and cultural changes in Europe. Almost all European countries have witnessed a rise in living standards, technological progress, a change in the economic structure (a shift from a manufacturing economy to a service and information economy), an increase in the level of educational attainment, together with cultural developments, such as secularisation, emancipation and individualisation. Particularly during the 2nd half of the 20th century, the situation of women changed significantly. Their participation in full-time education has risen sharply, resulting in an increased level of educational attainment and labour force participation by women, with serious implications for their economic situation. Women became increasingly economically independent of their male partners, which contributed to a postponement of marriage and motherhood. Living alone and unmarried cohabitation have become alternatives to marriage, at least at a certain stage of life.

Van de Kaa (1987) as well as Lesthaeghe and Surkyn (1988) assume that the second demographic transition is one common process in all European countries. According to a strict interpretation differences in family and fertility behaviour between countries are only temporary. According to this interpretation, differences in family and fertility behaviour between countries can be attributed to differences in timing. In some countries, changes in fertility and family behaviour started earlier than in other countries. If the latter countries are assumed to follow the same pattern of change with some delay, there will be convergence and it is thus assumed that differences between countries will shrink in the future. One alternative interpretation is that even though there are similarities in trends across countries, some differences between countries may be persistent, due to differences in the economic, social, and cultural context. For example, Blossfeld (1992) emphasises the importance of differences in preferences between Northern and Southern European countries (egalitarianism versus personal freedom). Moreover, there are important institutional differences (e.g. facilities for childcare).

Similar developments do not imply that differences will disappear. Kuijsten (1999) notes that one of the central elements of the Second Demographic Transition is a process of pluralisation of living arrangements and a decline in the institutionalisation of the life course. This leads to an increase in within-country diversity. It does not seem likely that this would result in a decrease in inter-country differences. In this interpretation of the Second Demographic Transition, similarities in trends do not result in the end of demographic diversity across European countries.

Any attempt to answer the question whether demographic trends are converging or whether inter-country differences are persistent requires an in-depth analysis of comprehensive data sets. It is not sufficient to analyse aggregate data. Changes in fertility and family behaviour are generated by a diffusion process. Innovating groups introduce new types of behaviour, such as unmarried cohabitation or voluntary childlessness. These groups especially include young, highly educated, urban, non-religious people (De Feijter, 1991). As other groups subsequently follow the example of the innovators, the new type of behaviour becomes more widespread. In the later stages of the process, as more groups adopt the new type of behaviour, the differences between sub-populations decline. Thus, an analysis of internal country differences is needed in order to identify the stage of the transition process. As a result, when comparing fertility and family behaviour between countries, it is important to assess differences between sub-populations, both within and between countries. Moreover, since changes over time are to be examined, differences between cohorts need to be analysed.

Comparative studies have shown important cross-national differences in family formation between Northern, predominantly Protestant countries and Southern, Roman Catholic countries. In the Northern European countries changes such as the decline in fertility and the increase in unmarried cohabitation started earlier than in the Southern European countries. One main problem in interpreting differences between Northern and Southern European countries is that many aspects of these societies differ. This makes it very difficult to identify individual causes of differences. For this reason a comparison of family formation in Belgium (= the Flemish Region and the Brussels Capital Region) and the Netherlands is particularly interesting. Whereas the religious denomination differs strongly between both countries, the economic and social differences are relatively small. Belgium is predominantly Roman Catholic, whereas the Netherlands has about equal proportions of Protestants and Roman Catholics. The economic system, living standards, geographical situation, and language are similar in both countries. Obviously a comparison of family formation in

Belgium and the Netherlands may provide useful insights in the nature of differences in the Second Demographic Transition across European countries.

Section 1.2 presents some aggregate data on the similarity and diversity in demographic trends in Belgium and the Netherlands (e.g. Anon, 1995a; 1995b; Beets et al., 1992; Eurostat, 1997; Latten, 1990). *Section 1.3* introduces both fertility and family surveys which provide the data that are analysed in this volume (e.g. Cliquet et al., 1992; Latten & de Graaf, 1997; Latten & Widdershoven, 1993; Lodewijckx, 1999). Finally, *section 1.4* gives a concise overview of the other chapters of this volume.

1.2 Demographic trends

The Netherlands and Belgium are the two most densely populated countries in the European Union. The population of the Low Countries totals 25 million people (Eurostat, 1997). Belgium has 10.1 million inhabitants. Looking at distribution among the regions, about 60% of the population live in Flanders, one third of the population in Wallonia and almost 10% in the Brussels Capital Region. The Netherlands has 15.5 million inhabitants. The difference in population size between Belgium and the Netherlands is increasing. In the first half of the 1990s the annual growth rate of the Dutch population was 0.7% on average, compared to 0.3% for the Belgian population. One main cause of the relatively high population growth in the Netherlands lies in the past. In the 1960s the Dutch fertility rate was considerably higher, now resulting in the higher percentage of women of childbearing age in the Netherlands. Consequently, the crude birth rate in the Netherlands is higher, even though the Total Fertility Rate (TFR) hardly differs between the Netherlands and Belgium. In addition, the annual number of immigrants in the Netherlands is higher and the life expectancy is slightly higher than in Belgium.

In the 1980s and 1990s the TFR both in Belgium and the Netherlands has fluctuated between 1.5 and 1.6 children per woman. In both countries, fertility rates among young women have dropped sharply since the 1970s. Teenage pregnancies have become rather rare. Fertility rates among older women have increased considerably. As a consequence, the mean age of childbearing has risen sharply. In the Netherlands the mean age for having the first child (over 28 years old) has risen to one of the highest levels in the world.

Over the past decades the level of fertility has dropped more strongly in the Netherlands than in Belgium. Dutch women born in 1935 had 2.5 children on average, Belgian women 2.3 children. In both countries, women born in 1950 had about 1.9 children. The percentage of women remaining childless is higher in the Netherlands than in Belgium: 10% of Belgian women and 15% of Dutch women born in 1950 have remained childless.

In Belgium and the Netherlands alike there has been a postponement of the age for leaving the parental home and of the age for the first marriage. However, these changes have been felt more strongly in the Netherlands than in Belgium. In 1995, 60% of Belgian women aged 25-29 years were married compared to only 44% of Dutch women. This difference is mainly due to the timing of marriage, given that the difference for the age group 30-39 years is much smaller: 75% of Belgian women aged 30-39 were married and 71% of Dutch women. The mean age of the first marriage has increased from 22.0 years in 1975 to 25.4 years in 1995 for Belgian women and from 22.6 years to 27.1 years for Dutch women.

The kind of living arrangement chosen at the time young adults leave the parental home is quite different between both countries (Corijn, 1996; Latten, 1996). In the Netherlands, marriage is no longer the main reason for leaving home, whereas in Belgium it remains the most prevalent pathway out of the parental home, although other pathways are becoming more widespread. About half of young Dutch adults, born in the second half of the sixties, have started living alone after leaving the parental home. The percentage of young women marrying without premarital cohabitation has declined sharply. Whereas the first partnership of 20% of Dutch women born around 1950 who entered into a partnership before they reached the age of 30 was a consensual union, the percentage has increased to 60% for women born around 1960. In Belgium, by contrast, postponement of the first marriage has so far not resulted in a strong increase in living alone or in unmarried cohabitation. Instead, young adults tend to stay longer in the parental home.

1.3 Fertility and family surveys

In the late 1980s the Population Activities Unit (PAU) of the United Nations Economic Commission for Europe (ECE) initiated a research programme focusing on fertility and family change. The objective of the programme is to conduct comparable Fertility and Family Surveys (FFS) in about 20 ECE member countries, to create standard files, to prepare standard country reports and to carry out cross-country comparative studies.

The present volume presents the results of a comparative study of fertility and family behaviour in Belgium and the Netherlands, mainly based on analyses of survey data gathered in the early 1990s. Both surveys followed the PAU recommendations. The questions cover childbirth, fertility regulation, labour force participation, childcare, partnership formation and a series of background variables. For Belgium, the Fertility and Family Survey (NEGO V) was conducted by the Population and Family Studies Centre (CBGS), in 1991 in the Flemish region and in 1992 in the Brussels region, among a representative sample of 5000 women and 3200 men born between 1951 and 1970. Since no such data collection is available for Wallonia, references to "Belgium" should be understood accordingly unless stated otherwise (e.g. *Chapter 2*). CBGS conducted the first Belgian Fertility survey in 1966 (e.g. Cliquet, 1985). For the Netherlands, the Fertility and Family Survey (OG'93) (*Onderzoek Gezinsvorming*) was conducted in 1993 by Statistics Netherlands (CBS), Department of Population, among a representative sample of 4500 women and 3700 men born between 1950 and 1974. OG'93 was the sixth Family and Fertility Survey organised by Statistics Netherlands; the first survey being held in 1974.

The *Technical Appendix* provides more detailed information, highlighting similarities and differences between both large surveys (Latten & de Graaf, 1997; Lodewijckx, 1999).

1.4 Summary of this volume

Van de Kaa (1997) identifies three major shifts in fertility and family behaviour that have occurred since the mid-60s: (1) changes in contraceptive behaviour; (2) changes in the level and pattern of fertility; (3) changes in the timing, frequency, type and stability of unions. In each of these areas a sequence of events can be discerned. He also claims that the introduction of effective means of contraception in the 1960s was the main cause of the onset of the chain of events that together constitute the second demographic transition. The first effect of modern contraception was a reduction in higher order births. Subsequently, the relationship between marriage and fertility became looser: people could marry younger without immediately having children. The age at which people married declined, while childbearing was postponed. As pre-marital pregnancies declined, so the number of 'shot-gun' weddings fell and the age at which people first married started to rise. In the 1970s, cohabitation became an easier option, which led to a further postponement of marriage and childbirth. Since the 1980s, cohabitation has increasingly become an alternative to marriage, at least temporarily. As a result, extra-marital fertility has risen (Van de Kaa, 1997).

The present volume aims to take stock of the current stage of the transition process in Belgium and the Netherlands. In analysing the three major shifts in fertility and family behaviour, attention is focused on the early stage of the life cycle. For this reason, the beginning of family formation, rather than the dissolution of partnerships is considered. In line with the sequence of events as described by Van de Kaa (1997), the analyses in *Chapter 2* document the changes in fertility regulation, especially contraceptive behaviour. *Chapter 3* includes analyses of changes at the beginning of the family formation process after leaving the parental home. The subsequent chapters examine changes in fertility. *Chapter 4* focuses on changes in the timing and level of fertility, whereas *Chapter 5* analyses the relationship between the fertility and labour force participation of women. Finally, *Chapter 6* presents a number of conclusions based on the findings of Chapters 2 to 5. As mentioned above, the *Technical Appendix* includes more detailed information about the two surveys which provide the core data under study in this volume.

Chapter 2 by de Graaf and Lodewijckx examines changes in the application of family planning in Belgium and the Netherlands. They report that the contraceptive transition was not identical in both countries. While in the early 1980s Dutch contraceptive practice was slightly more modern than that in Belgium, the differences between both countries have disappeared by the 1990s.

Chapter 3 by Corijn and Manting compares the choice of living arrangement after leaving the parental home. They conclude that in the Netherlands the propensity to marry started to decline earlier and, as a consequence, has reached a lower level than in Belgium. In this respect, the Netherlands may be considered a forerunner compared to Belgium. However, an examination of changes in the alternatives to marriage, i.e. living in a consensual union and living without a partner, leads to a less straightforward conclusion. As the percentage of young people entering into a consensual union has been rising moderately in Belgium in recent years, Belgium seems to be following the same pattern as the Netherlands. This, however, does not apply to the other alternative to marriage, living without a partner. The percentage of young people whose first move after leaving the parental home is to live without a partner for some time has increased sharply in the Netherlands. In Belgium, this type of behaviour still remains fairly uncommon. Whereas in the Netherlands young people tend to choose between living with or without a partner, young Belgians seem to choose between living with a partner or not yet leaving the parental home. Consequently, Belgium is not (yet) following the same path as the Netherlands.

Chapter 4 by de Jong and Lodewijckx examines fertility behaviour. In order to disentangle the effects of changes in the timing and level of fertility, both actual fertility and expectations about the ultimate number of children are analysed. During the 1980s, in Belgium and the Netherlands alike, there was a strong tendency to postpone childbearing. In the Netherlands, the average age for having the first child has increased more dramatically than anywhere else in Europe. By comparison, the mean age for becoming a mother is about one year earlier in Belgium than in the Netherlands. Differences in the postponement of motherhood are strongly related to the level of educational attainment. The average number of children per woman has declined more strongly in the Netherlands than in Belgium. Whereas Dutch women born before the Second World War had more children than Belgian women, the number of children per woman among post-war cohorts hardly differs.

Fertility is closely related to female labour force participation. One of the explanations for the postponement of childbirth is that women increasingly tend to have a paid job for some years before they decide to have children. On the other hand, fertility affects the female labour supply. In the Netherlands the labour force participation rate of mothers of young children has been much lower than in Belgium. *Chapter 5* by Callens, van Hoorn and de Jong concludes that over the past decade the percentage of women who do not leave their job after giving birth to their first child has risen strongly in the Netherlands. Nevertheless, the labour force participation rate of mothers of young children is still considerably lower than in Belgium. One may therefore consider Belgium as a forerunner compared to the Netherlands. It should, however, be noted that there is a much stronger tendency in the Netherlands to have a part-time job. The percentage of Belgian women with a part-time job has also risen, but the level still remains much lower compared to Dutch women.

One significant conclusion of *Chapter 6*, by de Beer, Corijn and Deven, is that some important differences remain in fertility and family behaviour between Belgium and the Netherlands, although they seem to have become smaller over the past two decades. Both countries, moreover, do not follow the same path. Many demographic trends seem to correspond to the concept of the second demographic transition (effective contraception, postponement of marriage and parenthood, increase in cohabitation), but the empirical findings suggest that not all the demographic differences between Belgium and the Netherlands can be interpreted in terms of the same transition process. Hence, we expect that some differences will persist between the two countries.

References

Anon (1995a), International Conference on Population and Development 1994: National Report submitted by the Belgian Government. In: H. van den Brekel and F. Deven (eds.), *Population and Family in the Low Countries. Selected Current Issues*. Dordrecht, Kluwer Academic Publ.: pp. 231-256. *(ESPO 2)*.

Anon (1995b), International Conference on Population and Development 1994: National Report submitted by the Dutch Government. In: H. van den Brekel and F. Deven (eds.), *Population and Family in the Low Countries. Selected Current Issues*. Dordrecht, Kluwer Academic Publ.: pp. 257-292. *(ESPO 2)*.

Beets, G., Y. Prins and P. Willems (1992), Trends in Population and Family in the Low Countries. *Bevolking en Gezin*, 92/1, pp. 77-99.

Blossfeld, H.P. (1992), Women's increasing educational attainment and changes in the process of family formation in Europe. Brusselss, Commission of the European Community.

Callens, M. (1995), De 'Fertility and Family Survey' in Vlaanderen (NEGO V, 1991). De gegevensverzameling. Brussels, *CBGS Document 4*.

Cliquet, R.L. (1985), Prognostische und politische Relevanz der CBGS-Erhebungen über das generative Verhalten. In: J. Schmid and K. Schwarz (eds.), *Politische und prognostische Tragweite von Forschungen zum generative Verhalten*, Deutsche Gesellschaft für Bevölkerungswissenschaft, Berlin, pp. 63-140.

Cliquet, R.L., F. Deven, M. Corijn, M. Callens, E. Lodewijckx (1992), Conceptual and analytical Framework of the 1991 Fertility and Family Survey in Flanders (NEGO V). Brusselss, *CBGS Werkdocument 82*.

Cliquet, R.L. and M. Callens (ed.) (1993), Gezinsvorming in Vlaanderen: Hoe en Wanneer? Brusselss, *CBGS Monografie 2*.

Corijn, M. (1996), *Transition into Adulthood. Results from the Fertility and Family Survey 1991-92*. The Hague/Brusselss, NIDI/CBGS Publications, vol. 32.

De Feijter, H. (1991), Voorlopers bij demografische veranderingen. The Hague: NIDI.

Eurostat (1997), Demographic statistics 1997, Luxembourg.

Kuijsten, A. (1999), Households, families and kin networks (87-122). In: L. van Wissen and P. Dykstra (eds.), *Population Issues. An Interdisciplinary Focus*. New York: Kluwer Academic/Plenum Publishers.

Latten, J.J., (1990), Jongeren bleven in jaren '80 weer langer bij hun ouders wonen. Ontwikkeling sinds de jaren '60, *Maandstatistiek Bevolking, CBS,* 10, pp. 14-24.

Latten, J.J. and M. Widdershoven (1993), The 1993 Fertility and Family Survey. pp. 75-79, In: *Netherlands Official Statistics. Population Statistics (Reprint 5)*. Voorburg: CBS.

Latten, J.J. and P.F. Cuyvers (eds.) (1994), *Relatie- en Gezinsvorming in de Jaren Negentig*. Voorburg, Centraal Bureau voor de Statistiek, Hoofdafdeling Bevolkingsstatistieken.

Latten, J.J. and A. de Graaf (1997), *Fertility and Family Surveys in Countries of the ECE Region. Standard Country Report. The Netherlands.* Geneva, UN/ECE Economic Studies No.10c.

Lesthaeghe, R., D. van de Kaa (1986), Twee demografische transities? pp. 9-24. In: R. Lesthaeghe and D. van de Kaa (eds.), *Groei of Krimp?* Deventer, Van Loghum Slaterus.

Lesthaeghe, R. And J. Surkyn (1988), Cultural dynamics and economic theories of fertility change. *Population and Development Review,* 14, pp. 1-45.

Liefbroer, A.C., M. Corijn, J. De Jong Gierveld (1996), *Similarity and diversity in the onset of family formation in the Low Countries.* Brussels, CBGS Document 3.

Van de Kaa, D. (1987), Europe's second demographic transition. Population Bulletin 42.

Van de Kaa, D. (1997), Options and sequences. Europe's demographic patterns. Nethur Working Paper No. 39.

Lodewijckx, E. (1999), Fertility and Family Surveys in Countries of the ECE Region. *Standard Country Report. Belgium.* Geneva: UN/ECE Economic Studies.

2. FERTILITY REGULATION

Arie de Graaf and Edith Lodewijckx

2.1 Introduction

Since the mid 1960s, certain aspects of partnership and reproductive behavioural patterns have demonstrated accelerated development in Western European countries, including Belgium and the Netherlands (Cliquet, 1991). Marriage has been postponed, divorce rates have increased, unmarried cohabitation and other living arrangements have become socially more acceptable (CBS, 1990; Corijn, 1993). People have become sexually active at a younger age (Lodewijckx, 1987a; Peters, 1992). In Belgium, for example, 16% of women born between 1946 and 1950 had sexual intercourse before their eighteenth birthday, compared with 24% and 29% of birth cohorts born in 1956-1960 and 1966-1970 respectively. Fertility dropped sharply and its pattern changed.
These changes were made possible by, among other things, the availability and use of modern contraceptives, enabling better planning of both the number and timing of births.

This chapter considers possible differences in birth control behaviour between Belgium and the Netherlands at the beginning of the nineties. It also examines to what extent the practice of birth control in the two countries changed during the 1980s. Special attention is paid to trends in sterilisation. Since fertility regulation also includes pregnancy termination, some data on abortion are also presented.

Most of the results presented in this chapter are from large fertility and family surveys (NEGO V for Belgium and OG'93 for the Netherlands). Information about these surveys, which cover the beginning of the 1990s, is given in the *Technical Appendix*. The results refer to women only, because men were not interviewed about contraception in the Netherlands. For informa-

J. de Beer and F. Deven (eds.), Diversity in Family Formation, 11–32.

tion about the surveys covering the early 1980s (NEGO IV and OG'82), the reader is referred to previous publications (Debusschere, 1985; CBS, 1984).

One final remark should be made concerning the survey population: as explained in Chapter 1 and in the Technical Appendix, Belgium is defined here as "Flanders + Brussels". This does not, however, apply to all analyses in this chapter. The comparison of the situation in 1982 with that in 1992 only includes women living in Flanders, since the former survey only covered this region. Fertility indicators were also calculated for Flanders, whereas abortion data are for the whole of Belgium, since a breakdown by region is impossible. For the sake of convenience, reference is made to Belgium in the text, but the exact delineation is specified in the tables.

2.2 Changes in fertility

Since the mid 1960s, fertility has declined sharply in Europe (Council of Europe, CDPO, 1997). Whereas Dutch women born in 1940 had had 2.2 children by the end of their reproductive period, those born in 1945 only had 2.0 and those born in 1950 1.9 (*Figure 2.1*). The two-child family became more and more popular and is by far the most common at present. Various surveys have demonstrated that women have been opting for fewer children in recent decades. Since the 1980s, a clear preference for two children has been noted in both countries (Callens & Deven, 1993; CBS, 1994a).

Alongside this decline, a shift in the fertility pattern was also observed. In the Netherlands, for example, fewer women under 29 were having children and more and more women aged between 29 and 44 were becoming pregnant. In Belgium, a similar shift was observed, with the turning point at the age of 27 (*Figure 2.2*).

Motherhood was increasingly being postponed. In 1980, the age of Dutch mothers giving birth to their first child was on average 25.6, and that of Belgian mothers 24.7. In 1993 it had risen to 28.0 and 26.6 years respectively (*Figure 2.3*).

Figure 2.1. Average number of children per woman in Belgium and the Netherlands (1935-1950)

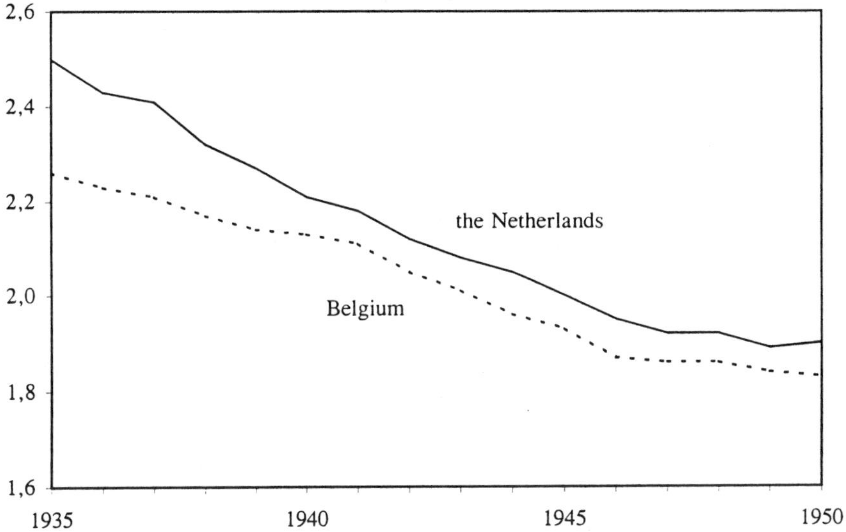

Source Belgium: CBGS, P. Willems, demographic databases (Belgium=Flanders)
Source the Netherlands: SN, Department of Population

These shifts all occurred at the same time as the increased availability of modern contraceptives (de Graaf, 1994; Lodewijckx, 1988). There is no doubt that these have played an instrumental role in family planning, through the prevention of unwanted pregnancies - both within and outside marriage and better planning of the timing of the births. The underlying motives for wanting fewer children and for changes in relational behaviour and reproductive patterns are connected to the prolonged education of women and their increased participation in the labour market (Cliquet, 1991; Davis et al., 1987; Romaniuc, 1990; Roussel, 1989).

Consequently, it is important to know how, how much and how effectively couples practise fertility regulation since this can affect both the timing and the intensity of fertility. As elsewhere in Europe, this theme was covered by the fertility and family surveys in Belgium and the Netherlands.

Figure 2.2.Age-specific fertility rates in Belgium and the Netherlands (1982, 1992)

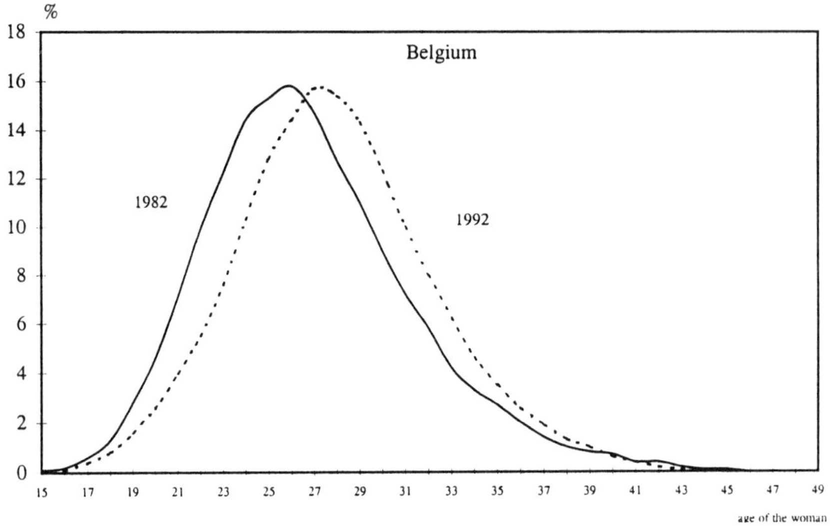

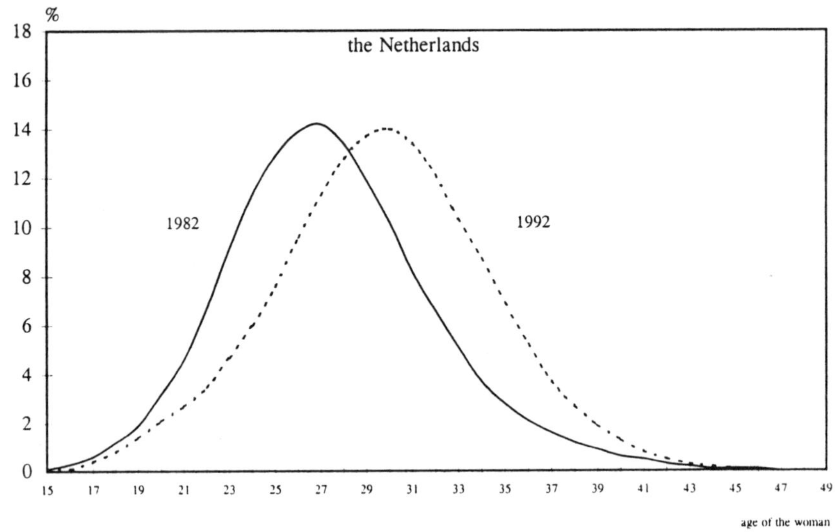

Source Belgium: CBGS, P. Willems, demographic databases (Belgium=Flanders)
Source the Netherlands: SN, Department of Population

Figure 2.3. Mean age of women having a first child in Belgium and the Netherlands (1980-1993)

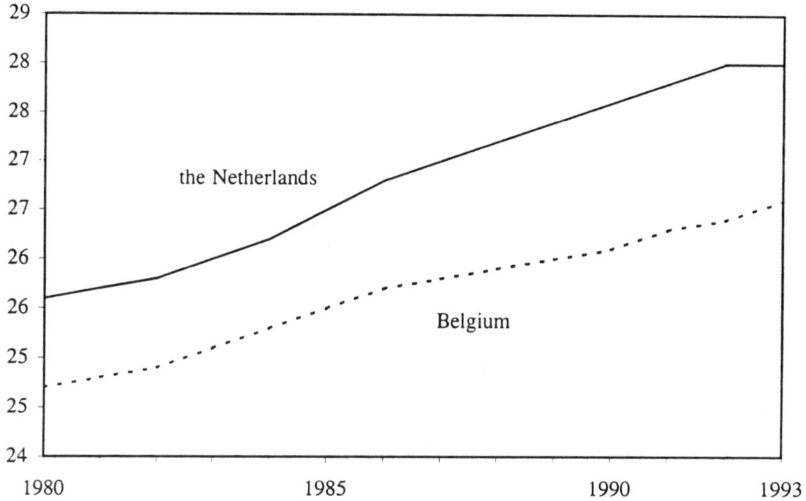

Source: Belgium: CBGS, P. Willems, demographic databases (Belgium=Flanders)
Source: The Netherlands: SN, Department of Population.

Recent surveys reveal considerable differences between individual (Western) European countries in overall contraceptive practice, the choice of methods and means and the incidence of abortion (Riphagen & Lehert, 1989; United Nations, 1989, 1992, 1993). Blayo (1993a) divides European countries into three groups by virtue of their birth control behaviour. Firstly, countries with high contraceptive use, mainly medical contraceptive methods. Here, abortion rates are low; pregnancy termination occurs only in cases of contraceptive failure; sterilisation is rare. The second group comprises countries where abortion rates are even lower; not because contraceptives are used more widely, but because more people undergo sterilisation. This group includes the Netherlands, Belgium and the United Kingdom. The third group comprises those countries (mainly in Eastern Europe) where abortion replaces contraception regularly or completely and where the number of sterilisations is negligible. In Romania, for example, an average of six abortions per woman can be observed (Blayo, 1993b).

All Western European countries experienced a contraceptive transition characterised by a shift from 'traditional', ineffective methods (coitus interruptus, periodic abstinence) to the predominant use of 'modern', medical and effective means (pill, IUD, sterilisation). The transition did not take place at the same time everywhere, and not always according to the same pattern.

Cliquet & Lodewijckx (1986) distinguished two groups of countries. In Anglo-Saxon countries and in North-Western Europe the transition occurred very early and barrier methods were an important link in the transition from traditional to modern methods. In Southern Europe a slower rate of change was observed, including a slow decline in the practice of coitus interruptus and/or the rhythm method, the late acceptance of hormonal, intra-uterine and surgical contraception, and low use of condoms and diaphragms. Although, from a geographical and economic point of view, Belgium and the Netherlands both belong to the Anglo-Saxon countries and North-Western Europe, the Netherlands had a contraceptive transition comparable with those countries, whereas the transition in Belgium more closely resembled that of the Southern European countries. Belgium (especially Flanders) was predominantly Roman Catholic, a fact which —alongside other factors (Deven, 1986)— certainly resulted in differences in mentality and legislation concerning family planning between Belgium and the Netherlands.

2.3 Method of birth control

2.3.1 Birth control in the early 1990s

Table 2.1 relates birth control to fecundity. Women who say they can have children (or at least have no reason to believe they cannot) are divided according to birth control practice and method or the reason for not using any method. The non-fecund women (couples) are divided according to the reason for infecundity: sterilisation or infertility (biological or due to illness, accident or surgical operation).

Birth control behaviour has become generally accepted in the Netherlands and in Belgium. Of all Belgian women aged 21-40 in the early nineties 74% were using a method to prevent pregnancy. Reasons for non-use were: pregnant or wanting to become pregnant (10%), no steady relationship or no sexual intercourse within the relationship (8%), infecundity of one or both partners, excluding sterilisation (5%) or other more specific reasons (3%). For the Netherlands, the corresponding percentages are very similar.

Table 2.1. Belgian and Dutch Women, by method of contraception in the early 1990s (in %)

Age at interview	Country	Fecund[1]							Fecund[2]			Total (abs. = 100%)
		No method of birth control			Contraceptive Method						Other	
		Pregnant or want to be pregnant	No relationship	Other reasons	Pill, injection	IUD	Condom	CI/PA[3]	Sterilization			
									Woman	Partner		
21-25	Belgium	11	16	2	63	1	4	1	0	0	2	785
years	the Netherlands	7	9	3	70	1	6	2	0	0	1	890
26-30	Belgium	17	6	4	51	4	5	3	4	2	5	958
years	the Netherlands	14	6	4	59	2	9	2	1	1	2	923
31-35	Belgium	8	5	4	40	8	5	5	12	8	6	946
years	the Netherlands	13	5	5	36	5	11	3	4	12	5	904
36-40	Belgium	3	6	4	26	7	5	5	27	12	6	737
years	the Netherlands	5	5	7	25	5	8	4	10	21	10	851
Total	Belgium	10	8	3	46	5	5	4	10	5	5	3426
(21-40 years)	the Netherlands	10	6	5	48	3	9	3	4	9	4	3568

1 For women living with husband or male friend: both fecund
2 For women living with husband or male friend: at least one of the partners infecund
3 Including other and unknown method of contraception

Source: CBGS, NEGO V-survey 1991 (Flanders) + FFS-survey 1992-93 (Brussels)
SN, Netherlands Fertility and Family Survey 1993

For young women, the non-use of contraceptives is mainly connected to pregnancy, the desire to become pregnant or the lack of a sexual relationship. The latter reason is more often reported by Belgian 21-25 year-olds than by their Dutch peers. The above-mentioned differences in the timing of births between Belgian and Dutch women are reflected in these figures. Relatively more Dutch women compared to Belgian women aged thirty or over are pregnant or want to become pregnant. This means that more Belgian women in this age group practise contraception (e.g. age 31-35: the Netherlands 71%, Belgium 78%). For older women, their own or their partner's infecundity also plays a role. Other reasons which make it unnecessary to use contraception are, for example, a recent birth, gynaecological complaints making the risk of pregnancy (temporarily) low or medical treatment incompatible with use of contraceptives. Both in Belgium and in the Netherlands less than 1% of 21-40 year-olds do not use contraceptives on ethical/religious grounds. In Belgium no fewer than 2% of women have a *laissez-aller* attitude: they use no form of contraception although they do not intend to have a(nother) child.

In addition to high overall use, the Belgian and Dutch populations are characterised by high application of modern methods. In both countries. the pill is by far the most popular form of contraception, with the exception of 36-40 year-olds. The youngest age group relies almost exclusively on oral contraceptives (*Table 2.2*). Due to its irreversible nature, sterilisation is more common among older age groups. Relatively more Belgian than Dutch women are sterilised. The opposite holds for men. The total proportion of sterilised respondents is slightly higher in Belgium. This probably relates to the fact that Dutch women have their children when they are slightly older than Belgian women. IUDs and other methods such as coitus interruptus (CI) and periodic abstinence (PA) are at the same level in both countries. Condom use is noted more often for the Netherlands.

2.3.2 Changes during the 1980s

In 1982, the contraceptive profiles for Belgium and the Netherlands showed a large degree of correspondence. Then, too, contraceptive methods were used by nearly all fecund women who had a relationship, without being or wanting to become pregnant. Predominantly modern methods were used. Relatively more Dutch women were sterilised.

Table 2.2. Woman who used a method of contraception, by method, in the early 1990s (in %)

Age at interview	Country	Pill, injection	IUD	Condom	CI/PA[1]	Sterilisation		Total (abs=100%)
						Woman	Partner	
21-25 years	Belgium	92	1	5	2	0	0	545
	The Netherlands	88	1	8	2	0	1	713
26-30 years	Belgium	75	5	7	4	5	4	653
	The Netherlands	79	3	12	3	2	2	691
31-35 years	Belgium	52	10	7	7	15	10	727
	The Netherlands	50	7	16	5	5	17	649
36-40 years	Belgium	32	8	6	6	32	15	602
	The Netherlands	35	7	11	5	14	29	619
Total (21-40 years)	Belgium	62	7	6	5	13	8	2527
	The Netherlands	64	4	11	4	5	12	2673

[1]Including other and unknown methods of contraception
Source: CBGS, NEGO V survey 1991 (Flanders)+FFS survey 1992-93 (Brussels).
SN, Netherlands Fertility and Family Survey 1993 (OG'93).

Except among 21-25 year-olds in both countries, the proportion of women who used no contraception during the 1980s remained unchanged, whereas the percentage of non-users decreased. In Belgium this percentage dropped from 40% in 1982 to 31% in 1991; in the Netherlands from 28% in 1982 to 19% in 1993. Moreover, a rise in the use of hormonal contraception was observed in both countries and among all age groups (*Figure 2.4*). This trend went hand in hand with a new generation of low dosage pills, with only slight side effects (Samsioe, 1991). The increasing postponement of child-birth may explain the prolongation of pill use. As for the rise in pill use among the youngest, one factor may be that the parents of young women are familiar with hormonal contraceptives; the pill is no longer taboo and thus more accessible for their daughters.

IUD use has dropped in both countries (*Figure 2.4*). This method lost ground especially among 20-30 year-olds. This appears to be related to the post-ponement of motherhood: any complications are more serious for women who have never been pregnant than for those who have (Population reports, 1982). Moreover, the possible negative consequences of the use of IUDs (bleeding, ectopic pregnancy, excessive and painful menstruation) apparently put many women off (Lodewijckx, 1987b).

The use of the condom increased in the Netherlands during the eighties, although mainly among 31-37 year-olds. In Belgium the percentage of condom users remained the same. Safe sex campaigns related to HIV/AIDS prevention have run in both countries. The effect of these campaigns cannot be established from these surveys, however, as the questions were targeted at the prevention of pregnancy, not the practice of safe sex. If the condom has gained ground in Belgium during the 1980s, it was in combination with the use of more effective methods such as oral, intra-uterine or surgical forms of contraception (in the survey only the modern method of contraception was noted, so there is no increase in condom use seen in *Figure 2.4*). In the Netherlands, on the other hand, it looks as if some condom users see the condom as a replacement for other forms of contraception, in spite of the recommended strategy of combined use (Van Zessen & Sandfort, 1991).

In Belgium, coitus interruptus and/or periodic abstinence declined further in both age groups, a continuation of the trend which had already been observed since the sixties (Cliquet & Lodewijckx, 1986). The percentage of Dutch couples using these traditional methods was already low in 1982 and hardly decreased any further during the eighties.

Surgical contraception fell sharply in the Netherlands, especially among women. This is connected with the trend of having children later in life. The age at which people undergo sterilisation has risen (see also *Section 2.3.3*). Moreover, the introduction of low-oestrogen oral contraceptives may have persuaded women to use these instead of undergoing sterilisation. It also seems that, among Dutch couples, men more often than women underwent the operation. As a result, at the beginning of the 1990s, the percentage of sterilised partners of women aged 31-37 years was three times that of sterilised women in that age group. In Belgium, sterilisation shows a completely different pattern. Overall, it increased among 31-37 year-olds. The percentage of men being sterilised rose from 4% to 14%, while that for women dropped slightly (from 23% to 20%). Still, more women than men underwent the operation.

2.3.3 Sterilisation

To elucidate the changed pattern of sterilisation, *Figure 2.5* shows the age-specific percentages of women who have been sterilised, including women with a sterilised partner, for various birth cohorts.

Figure 2.4. Belgian and Dutch women who used a contraceptive method by method and by age group in the early 1980s and 1990s (in %)

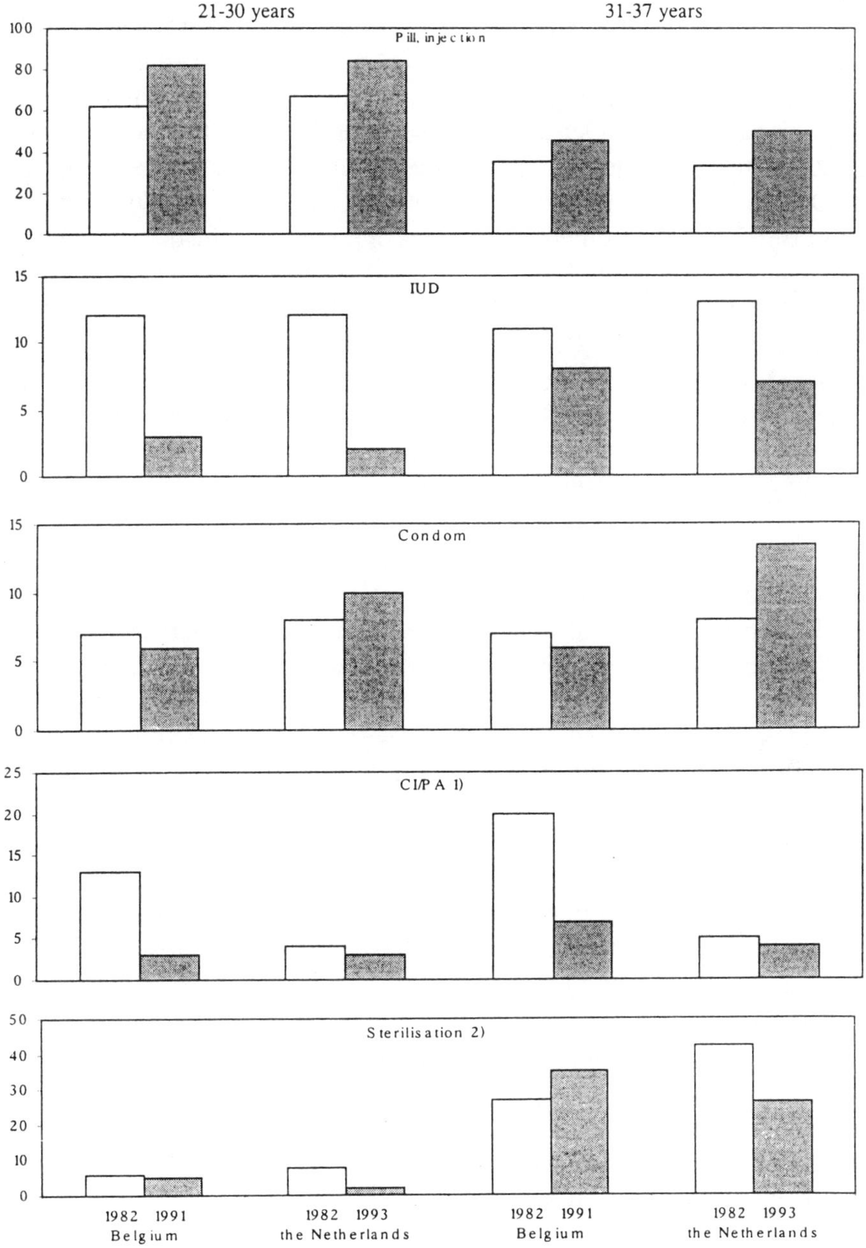

1) including other and unknown contraceptive method. 2) including partner
Source: Belgium CBGS, NEGO IV-survey 1982-83 + NEGO V-survey 1991 (Flanders)
Source: the Netherlands SN, Netherlands Fertility and Family Survey 1982 and 1993.

It appears that, in the Netherlands, following a period when operations took place at an increasingly younger age, starting with cohort 1951-1953 or certainly from cohort 1954-1956 the trend has been to postpone sterilisation. This trend may result in increased cancellation, since procrastination is the thief of time. Our surveys do not provide any information in this respect. In view of the increase in sterilisation in Belgium mentioned above during the nineteen-eighties, it is not surprising to see that the trend towards sterilisation at an increasingly younger age is still present in cohorts 1951-1953 and 1954-1956. Only for cohort 1957-1959 is there any indication of a possible break with the trend: fewer women had undergone sterilisation before their 32nd birthday than in the cohort 1954-1956. Since we asked Belgian women about their sterilisation intentions, we tend to expect that the percentage of those sterilised in cohort 1957-1959 will be higher than in cohort 1954-1956 at the same age (Lodewijckx, 1993b). Moreover there are no indications that this potential change in delaying the operation will lead to cancellation in cohort 1957-1959. The percentages of women (couples) who opt for sterilisation in cohort 1957-1959 will presumably be similar to those from the two preceding cohorts.

Why do couples choose sterilisation? Dutch mothers aged 31-40 who themselves or whose partner had opted for surgical contraception were asked for the underlying reasons or considerations. Sterilisation is seen as the most effective way to maintain the actual number of children. Of the women, 13% mentioned 'physical/mental' health as a reason for the operation. For most women, the other reply options were less important.

In Belgium, 31-40 year-olds who did not intend that either they themselves or their partners should undergo sterilisation were presented with a list of reasons to account for their preferences. The most impòrtant reason for not relying on surgical contraception was the availability of and satisfaction with other forms of contraception, making sterilisation unnecessary (mentioned by 84% of respondents). The irreversible nature of the operation put many off (57%). This is stressed more by younger than by older women (64% of 31-35 year-olds versus 48% of 36-40 year-olds). Both fear of the operation and the risk of possible side effects were mentioned by over a quarter of the women. One fifth of the women said they would no longer feel 'complete' after the operation. Less frequently mentioned reasons were the partner's objection (12%), unfamiliarity with the method (13%), or the idea that it was unhealthy (10%).

Figure 2.5. Percentage of Belgian and Dutch women who have been sterilised or whose partner has been sterilised, for various birth cohorts (in %).

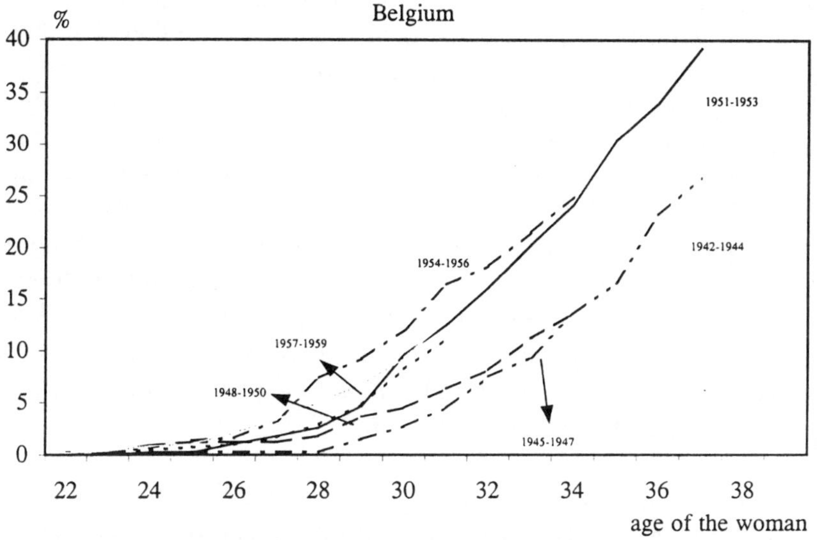

Source: CBGS, NEGO IV survey 1982-83 (Flanders) + NEGO V survey 1991 (Flanders)

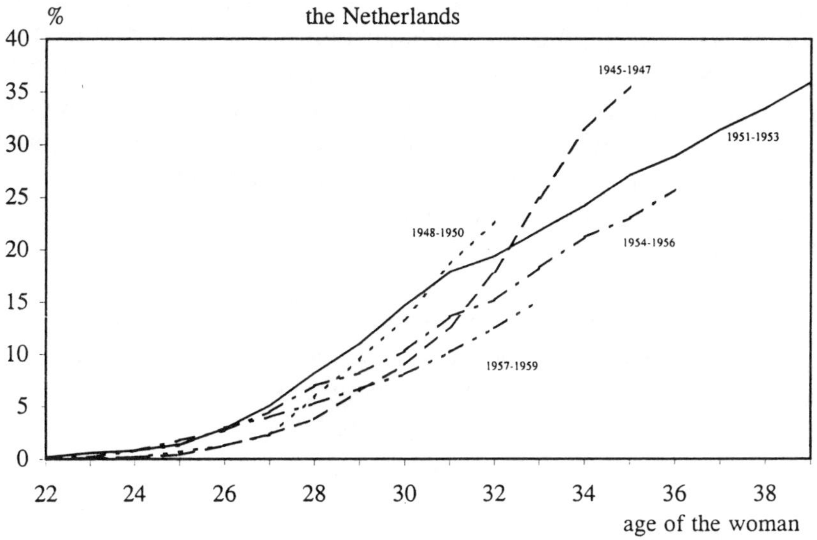

Source: SN, Netherlands Fertility and Family Survey 1982 and 1993.

2.4 Differences in contraceptive use

This section examines whether specific contraceptive methods are used more or less by women with certain characteristics. Data from previous surveys, both in Belgium and the Netherlands, show that some contraceptive methods were practised more by a certain group in the population than by another. From bivariate analyses of the OG'88 data it appears, for example, that mothers —who are generally older than women without children— mainly use the pill, the IUD or are sterilised. Women who regularly attend church services use the pill or sterilisation slightly less often. Relatively high numbers of churchgoers abstain from using contraception. The woman's educational level is also important: those with the lowest education are more likely to have completed their family and hence are sterilised more often. The most highly educated women mainly use the pill, IUD or condoms since they are still at the stage of family formation (Beets, 1989).

The multiple classification analysis (MCA, see *Technical Appendix*) of the Belgian NEGO IV data reveals that in 1982 various background characteristics (degree of urbanisation of residential municipality, educational level and religious denomination of the couple, partner's occupation and parity) are not very helpful in explaining whether modern contraceptives are used. Among 40-44 year-olds, however, religious denomination and parity are the most differentiating characteristics. Roman Catholics use the IUD, pill and sterilisation significantly less often than non-religious and latitudinarian women. Moreover, Catholic women differ according to Mass attendance, where women who attend church services most often use traditional methods. Furthermore, the lower the number of children, the less they use modern contraceptives (Lodewijckx & Impens, 1988).

Table 2.3 also shows that the variables included in the model explain to only a very small extent whether or not modern methods are used. In 1991 the differentiating effect of these social and demographic characteristics on the use of modern contraceptives had disappeared in Belgium. For Dutch women, they explain only 6% of the variation.

In the MCA analysis of the Belgian and Dutch data from the early 1990s, contraceptive methods are divided into two groups: 'traditional' versus 'modern'. The latter comprise hormonal, intra-uterine and surgical contraception. 'Traditional' methods are defined as: condoms, coitus interruptus, periodic abstinence and intra-vaginal devices. Women who reject contraception on moral grounds are also included in this group. Both in Belgium and in the Netherlands, about 85% of 21-40 year-old 'users' rely on modern methods (*Table 2.3*). This percentage decreases among older women.

The oldest women show a slight increase in both countries, due to the increase in sterilisation. The most important differentiating variable for the choice of a modern versus a traditional method is the woman's age (beta = 0.15 and 0.12 respectively). The differentiation by age (eta = 0.09) observed in the bivariate analysis increases slightly after controlling for the other social and demographic characteristics. In comparing both countries it is notable that the characteristics 'level of education', 'church attendance' and 'live-born children' only have a differentiating effect in the Netherlands. A remarkable phenomenon is the relatively low use of modern methods by Dutch women with a high level of education, women who go to church regularly and women with one child. The relatively low use of modern methods by women with high educational level is related to a relatively high use of condoms. Furthermore the effect of the variable 'completed family' increases after correction. This holds true for women in both countries. It then becomes clear that women who have completed their family relatively frequently use a modern method.

2.5 Abortion

Although abortion legislation in the Netherlands only came into effect in 1984, the medical operation became widely established from the end of the sixties. STIMEZO, a foundation for pregnancy termination under medical supervision, started its permanent registration of out-patient abortions in 1974.

In Belgium, many efforts were made to change the very restrictive abortion legislation in force since 1970 (Deven, 1986), but it was only in 1990 that a new abortion law was introduced. Until then there had been a certain liberalisation, mostly in the Brussels region. In Flanders, where at that time there were hardly any abortion clinics, abortion 'tourism' by Belgian women to the Netherlands was a well-known phenomenon. As Dutch registration reveals, it still continues, albeit to a lesser extent, even after the introduction of the new Belgian law. Since the law of 1990 provides for compulsory registration, Table 2.4. gives the 1993 data, supplemented with data from Dutch registration.

In the Netherlands, pregnancy terminations among 15-44 year-old women dropped from 6.2‰ in 1980 to 5.6‰ in 1992 (CBS, 1994b). In Belgium too there was probably a decline. In 1980, the rate was presumably between 6.3‰ and 7.3‰ (the estimated number of abortions being 13,000 to 15,000; Verheye, 1981). In 1985 it was probably 7.5‰ (United Nations, 1992). In 1993 it was 6.0‰. In the early 1990s, abortion rates in Belgium and the Netherlands were low compared to European countries such as Germany (1990) 8.7‰; Italy (1990) 12.7‰; France (1988) 13.2‰; Lithuania (1990) 30.1‰; Norway (1990) 16.7‰; Hungary (1990) 40.0‰ (United Nations, 1992, 1993).

The abortion figures mentioned above include both native and immigrant women. From Dutch data it is apparent that the abortion rate for the native population is much lower than that for other ethnic groups. In 1990, for example, the rate was 5.2‰ among 15-44 year-old women living in the Netherlands; for native Dutch women the rate was 3.4‰ (Rademakers, 1992). For Belgium, such figures are not available at the moment.

The low abortion rates are certainly associated with the generally high level of effective family planning. However, there is no such thing as perfect contraceptive practice. Although both Belgium and the Netherlands have an established network for the provision of contraceptives, it is possible that some women, especially young or immigrant women, do not know how or where to obtain contraceptives or are deterred by the idea of having to consult a doctor first (Geeraert, 1988; Lodewijckx 1993a). Moreover, every form of contraception method has it own particular correct way of use; this may be difficult in some situations, or some women or their partners may not be aware of this (Impens & Lodewijckx, 1988; Rademakers and Ravesloot, 1993). Lastly, even reliable forms of contraception cannot completely exclude the risk of unplanned pregnancy. All these factors mean that unwanted pregnancies occur. Abortion may be considered as a correction and complement to the deficiencies of contraception. The low abortion rate makes it clear that abortion is not seen as a replacement for contraception. Abortion recidivism is low in both countries, certainly among native women (nearly 20%) (Kollektief Anticonceptie, 1994; Rademakers, 1992).

Table 2.3. Belgian and Dutch Women (21-40 year-olds) using a modern method of contraception, expressed as a percentage of all users[1]

	Belgium			The Netherlands		
	Unadjusted	Adjusted	Number of women	Unadjusted	Adjusted	Number of women
Grand mean	87		2588	84		2695
Age-group						
- 21-25 years	92	96	533	89	90	718
- 26-30 years	87	88	646	85	86	696
- 31-35 years	84	82	722	79	79	651
- 36-40 years	86	83	584	83	81	626
	eta=.09	beta=.15		eta=.09	beta=.12	
Cohabiting or not (married or unmarried)						
- yes	86	86	2064	84	85	1990
- no	90	88	420	84	82	701
	eta=.04	beta=.02		eta=.00	beta=.04	
Level of education						
- low	85	85	700	88	88	968
- medium	88	88	932	85	84	1272
- high	87	87	853	75	75	451
	eta=.04	beta=.03		eta=.12	beta=.12	
Church attendance						
- no religion	90	90	474	85	85	1095
- seldom or never	87	87	679	88	88	784
- sometimes	86	86	783	85	86	454
- regular	84	84	549	72	72	358
	eta=.05	beta=.05		eta=.14	beta=.13	
Live-born children						
- 0	89	87	751	87	88	1257
- 1	85	86	535	78	77	355
- 2+	86	87	1198	83	82	1079
	eta=.04	beta=.02		eta=.09	beta=.10	
Completed family size						
- yes	87	90	1496	85	89	1194
- no	86	82	988	84	81	1496
	eta=.01	beta=.12		eta=.02	beta=.11	
Municipality of residence						
- large	85	85	240	85	86	313
- medium	89	88	237	81	80	449
- small	87	87	2008	85	85	1929
	eta=.03	beta=.02		eta=.04	beta=.05	
Multiple R^2		0.020			0.055	

[1] including women rejecting contraception on moral grounds.

In the early 1990s, slightly fewer abortions were performed per 1,000 Dutch women than per 1,000 Belgian women *(Table 2.4.)*. In both countries the rates were highest for women aged 20-29 and lowest for those aged 40-44. The lower figures in the older age groups are linked to the high percentage of sterilisations. On the other hand, the decrease in potential fertility with age (Frank et al.,1994) is probably also important in this respect. The lower abortion rate in the youngest age group is, among other things, connected to the fact that many 15-19 year-olds are not yet sexually active.

Table 2.4. Induced abortions[1] in 1990/1993 Belgium/the Netherlands)

	Age distribution		Abortion rate		Abortion ratio	
	Belgium [2 3]	The Netherlands	Belgium [2]	The Netherlands	Belgium [2 4]	The Netherlands
	1993	1990	1993	1990	1993	1990
	%		per 1000 women		per 100 pregnancies [5]	
< 15 years	0.3	0.2	-	-	-	-
15-19 years	12.1	11.6	5.2	4.0	46.7	39.2
20-24 years	25.6	23.8	9.5	7.1	14.3	14.3
25-29 years	24.3	24.6	8.1	7.2	5.3	5.6
30-34 years	20.4	20.1	6.7	6.2	7.0	5.1
35-39 years	13.2	13.7	4.6	4.5	16.8	11.0
40-44 years	3.8	5.6	1.4	1.8	28.3	27.0
45 +	0.3	0.4				
Total	100	100	6 [6]	5.2 [6]	9.5 [6]	8.5 [6]
Absolute	12877 [7]	15697 [8]				

[1] For The Netherlands: Including menstrual regulation (termination of a pregnancy up to 16 days after menstruation failed to occur).
[2] Belgium = Flanders + Brussels + Wallonia.
[3] Based on the age distribution of induced abortions performed in Belgium
[4] Births by age of the mother: SPE data for Flanders (66,779 births in 1993, CBGS demographic database). For Belgium the same distribution is assumed.
[5] Pregnancies = live births + stillbirths + abortion.
[6] Computed per 1000 women aged 15-44 years.
[7] Induced abortions performed in Belgium (10,380) and performed in the Netherlands (2497).
[8] Women living in the Netherlands.

The age-specific abortion ratios, i.e. abortions per 100 known pregnancies (= live births + stillbirths + abortions) show a different pattern. In both countries, 15-19 year-olds score the highest. In Belgium, nearly half of 15-19 year-old women who became pregnant in 1993 had their pregnancy terminated. Among Dutch women in this age group there were apparently more wanted or accepted pregnancies. The same holds true for 35-39 year-old Dutch women, which is in accordance with the postponement trend described above.

2.6 Summary and conclusions

Like other European countries (Calot, 1990), Belgium and the Netherlands were characterised by very low fertility in the 1990s. The age-specific fertility rates show a rising trend at increased ages in both countries and the age at which women have their first child increased gradually during the 1980s. Fertility regulation is therefore very important in a couple's life. It is generally accepted, so much so in fact that the classic question 'Why do men and women use contraception?' has been replaced by the question 'Why are some people not using contraception?' Contraceptive practice has become the social norm and non-use is seen as deviant behaviour; indeed non-practice is only considered acceptable if a couple plans to have a child.

The Netherlands has been described as a 'perfect' family planning country (Beets, 1989). This can now also be said of Belgium. While in the early 1980s, the Dutch contraceptive profile was slightly more modern than that of Belgium, the contraceptive transition did not take place identically in both countries (Cliquet & Lodewijckx, 1986). The differences between Belgium and the Netherlands have now almost disappeared, with both countries now characterised by a high percentage of users, most of whom use the pill, and high sterilisation rates. The differentiating effect of classic social background characteristics on the use of contraceptives, and on modern forms in particular, has (nearly) disappeared. Abortion rates are among the lowest in the world.

Adolescents were not included in the surveys described here. Do 15-19 year-olds have the same favourable birth control profile as adults? In the 1980s the Netherlands was considered to be the country with the lowest relative number of teenage pregnancies and abortions in the world (Jones et al., 1986). Compared with young people from other countries, Dutch adolescents seem to be very skilled in preventing (unwanted) pregnancies. The high use of effective contraception is the most important explanation for this (Rademakers, 1991). Young Dutch people do not have less sexual intercourse nor do they start having sex later than their peers in other countries and there are no indications that Dutch teenagers are less fertile. In 1987 5.2‰ births and 4.0‰ abortions (i.e. 9.2‰ pregnancies) were recorded among 15-19 year-olds. About three-quarters of young people use the pill and/or condoms when they have sexual intercourse for the first time, while nearly one quarter uses no contraception, or at least no reliable form of contraception (including coitus interruptus or the rhythm method). For subsequent sexual intercourse, the level of reliable contraception was significantly higher, i.e. 90% (Rademakers, 1991). For Belgium, we estimate 5.9‰ births and 5.2‰ abortions among 15-19 year-olds. For 1989, Visser et al. (1991) noted that 23% of sexually active 15-19 year-old Belgian girls did not use any means of contraception, 61% used the pill, 12% used condoms and 4% practised coitus interruptus and/or the rhythm method.

Many factors have contributed to the remarkable success of fertility regulation in Belgium and the Netherlands, although it is difficult to determine the effect of each one individually. Moreover, the influence of each factor is not necessarily the same in both countries. The quality of family planning and contraceptive use is determined, for instance, by the availability of contraceptives, access to assistance in this field and knowledge of contraception and the motivation to practise it.
Availability is not a problem in Belgium or the Netherlands. Both countries have tried to remove the barriers people may experience in seeking assistance in the area of family planning: in the Netherlands, via general practitioners and the Rutgers foundation; in Belgium, where, compared to the Netherlands, medical specialists are more easily accessible, gynaecologists are the main providers of contraception. Moreover, contraception costs are reimbursed in both countries. The training of the services concerned -in this case doctors- is also important for the availability of the means. In both Belgium and the Netherlands, for example, low use of the IUD and high use of the pill were partly due to the fact that GP training did not include the insertion of IUDs - this was the reserve of gynaecologists; for a long time it was not even included in the training of gynaecologists in Belgium either, so that women were prescribed hormonal contraceptives if they wanted to use a form of modern contraception (Ketting, 1990; Lodewijckx & Deven, 1985).

Both countries have invested in information campaigns and sex education programmes, in which schools have played a considerable role. The media too have been an important and positive agent in this respect. Finally, regular research has been undertaken into the contraceptive behaviour of both populations, providing more insight into the possibilities of preventing unwanted pregnancies.

References

Beets, G.C.N. (1989), Geboortenregeling in Nederland, 1982 en 1988. CBS, *Maandstatistiek van de Bevolking*, 37, 1, pp. 21-27.

Blayo, C. (1993a), Family planning in Europe. *Entre Nous*, 22-23, pp. 3.

Blayo, C. (1993b), Access to abortion: The legal context, practice and frequency of recourse. *Entre Nous*, 22-23, pp. 6-9.

Callens, M. and F. Deven (1993), Kindertal: ideaal en wens. 97-122. In: R.L. Cliquet, M. Callens (eds.) *Gezinsvorming in Vlaanderen*. CBGS Monografie 1, Brussels.

Calot, G. (1990), La fécondité en Europe: Evolutions passées et perspectives d'avenir. *Bevolking en Gezin*, 3, pp. 56-82.

CBS (1984), *Onderzoek Gezinsvorming 1982. Verantwoording en uitkomsten*. The Hague: Staatsuitgeverij.

CBS (1990), *Onderzoek Gezinsvorming 1988. Samenwonen, trouwen, geboortenregeling, werken en kinderen krijgen*. The Hague: SDU/uitgeverij.

CBS (1994a), *Relatie- en gezinsvorming in de jaren negentig*. Centraal Bureau voor de Statistiek (Statistics Netherlands), Voorburg/Heerlen.

CBS (1994b), *Vademecum gezondheidsstatistiek Nederland*. Centraal Bureau voor de Statistiek (Statistics Netherlands), Ministerie van welzijn, volksgezondheid en cultuur. Voorburg/Heerlen/Rijswijk.

Cliquet, R.L. (1991), The Second Demographic Transition: Fact or Fiction? *Population Studies, 23*, Strasbourg: Council of Europe.

Cliquet, R.L. and E. Lodewijckx (1986), The contraceptive transition in Flanders. *European Journal of Population*, 2, pp. 71-84.

Corijn, M. (1993), *Leefvormen in Vlaanderen*. CBGS Monografie 2, Brussels.

Council of Europe (1997), *Recent demographic trends in Europe*. Strasbourg: Council of Europe.

Davis, K., M.S. Bernstam and R. Ricardo-Campbell (1987), *Below-Replacement Fertility in Industrial Societies*. Causes, Consequences, Policies. Cambridge: Cambridge University Press.

Debusschere, R. (1985), *De enquête "Gezinsontwikkeling in Vlaanderen 1982-1983". Technisch Verslag*. CBGS working document, 16, p. 67.

Deven, F. (1986), Planned Parenthood Legislation and Practice in Belgium. In: P. Meredith, L. Thomas (eds.), *Planned Parenthood in Europe. A Human Rights Perspective*. London: Croom Helm, pp. 135-162.

Frank, O., Bianchi, P.G. and A. Campana (1994), The end of fertility: age, fecundity and fecundability in women. *Journal of Biosocial Science*, 26, pp. 349-417.

Geeraert, A. (1988), Anticonceptie bij adolescenten. Een overzicht van gedrag, zingeving en normering tussen 1975 en 1985 18-36. In: E. Lodewijckx (ed.), *Gezinsplanning in Vlaanderen*. CBGS Monografie, 3.

Graaf, A. de (1994), Tweederde van de jonge vrouwen gebruikt de pil. In: Statistics Netherlands, *Maandstatistiek van de Bevolking*, 42/2, pp. 15-19.

Impens, K.K. and E. Lodewijckx (1988), Effectiviteit van de voorbehoeding. In: E. Lodewijckx (ed), *Gezinsplanning in Vlaanderen*. CBGS Monografie, 3, pp. 60-82.

Jones, E. et al. (1986), *Teenage pregnancy in industrialized countries*. New Haven/London: Yale University Press.

Ketting, E. (1990), Family planning in Western Europe: An overview of major issues. 1-12. In: Ketting, E. (ed.) *Contraception in Western Europe. A current appraisal*. Carnforth, Lancs: The Parthenon Publishing Group Inc.

Kollektief Anticonceptie (1994), *Jaarverslag 1993*. Ghent.

Lodewijckx, E. (1987a), First intercourse, contraception and first pregnancy in Flanders. Changes during the past 30 years. *Journal of Biosocial Science*, 19, 439-452.

Lodewijckx, E. (1987b), La perception des contraceptifs et quelques données sur la discontinuation. *Contraception - fertilité - sexualité*, 15, 11, pp. 1025-1030.

Lodewijckx, E. (ed.) (1988), *Gezinsplanning in Vlaanderen*. CBGS Monografie 3, Brussels.

Lodewijkcx, E. (1993a), *Geboortenregelend gedrag bij Turkse vrouwen in Vlaanderen en Brussel*. Working Paper "Etnische Minderheden in België", 1. Brussels.

Lodewijckx, E. (1993b), Vrijwillige sterilisatie van vrouw en man in Vlaanderen, anno 1991. *Tijdschrift voor Geneeskunde*, 49, 18, pp. 1237-1243.

Lodewijckx, E. and F. Deven (1985), *Het profiel van het IUD-gebruik in Vlaanderen*, 1982-1983. Brussels, CBGS werkdocument, 17

Lodewijckx, E. and K. Impens (1988), Bestaan er anno 1982-1983 nog differentiaties in het gebruik van anticonceptiva? pp. 104-117. In: Lodewijckx, E. (ed.), *Gezinsplanning in Vlaanderen*. CBGS Monografie, 3, Brussels.

Peters, E.W. (1992), *Veranderingen in de jeugdfase van meisjes. Generaties vergeleken*. DSWO Press, Rijksuniversiteit Leiden.

Population reports (1982), *Intrauterine devices*. Population reports, B4: B101-B135.

Rademakers, J. (1991), *Anticonceptie en interaktie. De preventie van ongewenste zwangerschap door jongeren in Nederland*. RU Utrecht, unpublished thesis.

Rademakers, J. (1992), *Abortus in Nederland 1989/1990. Jaarverslag van de landelijke abortusregistratie*. Utrecht: Stimezo.

Rademakers, J. and J. Ravesloot (1993), Jongeren en seksualiteit. 260-278. In: Dieleman A.J. et al. (eds.), *Jeugd in meervoud. De Tijdstroom*, Heerlen: Open Universiteit.

Riphagen, F.E. and P. Lehert (1989), A survey of contraception in five West European countries. *Journal of Biosocial Science*, 21, pp. 23-46.

Romaniuc, A. (1990), Réflexions sur le devenir démographique des sociétés avancées: un regard sur le Canada. *Cahiers Québecois de Démographie*, 19, 2, pp. 179-195.

Roussel, L. (1989), *La famille incertaine*. Paris: Jacob.

Samsioe, G. (ed.) (1991), *The pill: the most misunderstood drug in the world*. Proceedings of a symposium in Helsinki, Finland, June 1990. Carnforth: Parthenon.

United Nations (1989), *Levels and Trends of Contraceptive Use As Assessed in 1988*. Population Studies No 110. New York.

United Nations (1992), *Abortion Policies. A Global Review*. Volume I, Afghanistan to France. New York.

United Nations (1993), *Abortion Policies. A Global Review*. Volume II, Gabon to Norway. New York.

Van Zessen, G. and Th. Sandfort (1991), *Seksualiteit in Nederland; seksueel gedrag, risico en preventie van AIDS*. Amsterdam/Lisse: Swets and Zeitlinger.

Verheye, C. (1981), *Analyse van de poliklinische zwangerschapsonderbrekingen bij Belgische vrouwen in Nederland op grond van gegevens afkomstig van de Permanente Registratie*. Brussels: CBGS report 44.

Verslag Nationale Commissie (1994), Nationale Commissie voor de evaluatie van de wet van 3 april 1990 betreffende de zwangerschapsafbreking. Report for the Belgian Parliament. Brussels, August 1994.

Visser, A. Ph., A. Geeraert and P. Lehert (1991), *Seksualiteit en relatievorming. Anticonceptie in België*. Leuven/Amersfoort: Acco.

3. THE CHOICE OF LIVING ARRANGEMENT AFTER LEAVING THE PARENTAL HOME

Martine Corijn and Dorien Manting

3.1 Introduction

Leaving the parental home marks the onset of a young adult's own household career. The main reason for leaving the parental home used to be marriage. Nowadays, other reasons for leaving home, such as participating in education or getting a job, and other living arrangements such as cohabitation and living independently, have become more common. The age for leaving the parental home is related, among other things, to the reason for leaving or the living arrangement after flying the nest.

In the Netherlands, young adults who leave the parental home to live without a partner are on average younger than those who leave to live with a partner (De Jong Gierveld et al., 1991; Mulder & Manting, 1994, Mulder & Hooimeijer, 1995, Visser, 1994). Education or finding a job are important reasons for leaving home at early ages (Baanders et al., 1989; Mulder, 1993; Visser, 1994).

Both the timing of and reasons for leaving the parental home have been subject to change over time. The age for leaving the parental home continued to fall in most Western European countries until it stabilised or started to increase for the 1950 and 1960 cohorts (Latten, 1990; De Jong Gierveld & Liefbroer, 1992; Weick, 1992; Wagner & Huinink, 1991).

J. de Beer and F. Deven (eds.), Diversity in Family Formation, 33–58.

Changes in the route chosen for leaving the parental home are visible in many Western European countries, although at different levels. In the Netherlands, marriage is no longer the main reason for leaving the parental home, whereas in Belgium it remains so, although other reasons are gaining in popularity (Corijn, 1993; Mulder & Manting, 1994).

Family background and individual characteristics play a role in the timing and reason for flying the nest (Corijn, 1995; De Jong Gierveld et al., 1991; Mayer & Wagner, 1986; Weick, 1992; Goldscheider & Da Vanzo, 1989; Mulder & Manting, 1994; Mulder & Hooimeijer, 1995). A Roman Catholic background, for example, slows down the process of leaving home and encourages the traditional route of marriage.

The goal of this chapter is to examine differences in the timing of and the route for the process of leaving home between Belgium and the Netherlands. The focus will be on cohort and age-specific differences in the effect of the family background on leaving home. In the following section, a discussion of the theoretical background leads to the formulation of hypotheses. After a short description of the data and the method used (*section 3.3*), the empirical results are presented in *section 3.4*. The chapter ends with a discussion.

3.2 Theoretical background

Until the 1960s, marriage fluctuations were the main cause for changes in the timing of leaving home. As new living arrangements and other reasons for leaving home emerged and developments in marriage were thus no longer the sole explanation for fluctuations in leaving home (Goldscheider & Da Vanzo, 1989; Wagner & Huinink, 1991), so researchers began to study other ways of flying the nest.

Leaving home coincides with different living arrangements or is based on different reasons simultaneously. Until now, there has been little agreement about the way one should distinguish between the different routes out of the parental home. De Jong Gierveld et al. (1991) divide the reasons for leaving home into three categories: (1) to live with a partner, (2) to study or work elsewhere and (3) the desire for autonomy, privacy and independence. Individuals may feel, however, that the route to marriage is also the route to independence. Finding a job might also coincide with marriage. To study the process of leaving home, it is best to avoid overlapping reasons for leaving home. Other distinctions in the study of young adults flying the nest, where reasons did not overlap, were for instance, living unmarried in a house or apartment and living in shared accommodation, alone or with relatives (Goldscheider & Da Vanzo, 1989); leaving the parental home in order to live with a partner or without a partner (Visser, 1994; Mulder & Hooimeijer, 1995) and whether or not leaving the parental home coincided with marriage (Corijn, 1995; Mayer & Wagner, 1986; Weick, 1992).

An empirical argument for studying leaving home, taking different household outcomes into account, is that the factors that enhance marriage deter cohabitation (Blom, 1994; Liefbroer, 1991; Manting, 1994). In addition, Mulder and Manting (1994) found that behaviour during the period following leaving home of those who leave home via the traditional route - marriage - is quite different from the behaviour of those who leave home via the 'modern' routes - cohabitation and/or leaving home without a partner. In this study, non-overlapping routes for leaving home, focusing on the living arrangements young adults choose when they fly the nest are analysed. Three routes for leaving home are distinguished: leaving home to marry, to cohabit or to live without a partner.

Life course theory postulates that the individual life course is a sequence of changing personal experiences in the past and in the present which have become closely intertwined (Mayer & Tuma, 1990; Runyan, 1984). The family in which they grow up is an important determinant of the subsequent life cycle of children. It is a context defining economic, social and psychological costs and benefits which play a role in the child's decision to leave home.
The impact of parental (or the father's) education has been studied, taking the reasons for leaving home into account in countries such as the Netherlands, former West Germany and the USA (De Jong Gierveld et al., 1991; Mayer & Wagner, 1986; Weick, 1992; Goldscheider & Da Vanzo, 1989). Mayer and Wagner (1986) and Weick (1992) did not notice any significant impact of the educational characteristics of parents on their children leaving home, irrespective of coincidence with marriage. Goldscheider and Da Vanzo (1989), however, found that young people leave home earlier in families with higher parental education. With regard to the specific routes, parental education decreased the likelihood of leaving via marriage, but increased the likelihood of leaving home via other routes. De Jong Gierveld et al. (1991) showed that children more often leave home for reasons linked to independence, work or education if their father has a higher level of educational attainment. But it does not affect the process of leaving home to live with a partner. This might be due to the fact that the authors did

not make any distinction between leaving home to marry or cohabit. A few studies have shown that determinants hindering entry into marriage might sometimes stimulate entry into cohabitation in such a way that it has no effect at all on entry into a union, irrespective of the type of union (Liefbroer, 1991; Manting, 1994).
Parental education is associated with the level of financial resources, the learning environment at home and the educational or consumer aspirations to which children have been exposed (Axinn & Thornton, 1992; De Jong Gierveld et al., 1991; Liefbroer et al., 1993, Goldscheider & Waite, 1987). These characteristics, in turn, may affect children's decisions to leave home in a certain way and at a certain time. De Jong Gierveld et al. (1991) argue, for instance, that children who have a father with a high educational level are more likely to receive a more modern upbringing in which independence and autonomy are more highly valued. Higher educational aspirations for their children are supposed to influence children to postpone marriage and concentrate on achieving higher educational goals (Axinn & Thornton, 1992).
As such, the expectation in this study is that young adults who have parents of high educational attainment are less likely to leave home in the traditional way (via marriage) but are more eager to leave home via the more "modern" routes (cohabitation or living without a partner).

Another parental resource often studied is that of the religious environment in which a person was raised. Religiousness is strongly related to demographic behaviour. People who grow up in a strongly religious family themselves have traditional family values, leading them to choose the traditional life styles.
Weick (1992) found that women from Roman Catholic families left their parental home later. For men, there was no such relationship. De Jong Gierveld et al. (1991) also found that young adults who grew up in a family where religion was important left the parental home later to live together with a partner. They did not find such a relationship for those who left home alone. Goldscheider and Da Vanzo (1989) found that Roman Catholics and Jews are much less likely than Protestants to leave the parental home.
The expectation with respect to church attendance and leaving home in this study dictates that the more closely the parents are linked to a church, the more likely their children are to leave the parental home in the traditional way and the less likely they are to leave via other routes.

Life course theorists acknowledge that the individual life course is embedded in a historical context (Mayer & Tuma, 1990). People born in different periods face different historical conditions and are exposed to different norms, beliefs, attitudes and values (Ryder, 1965; Lesthaeghe & Moors, 1992). Several studies have shown that determinants have different influences on demographic behaviour according to the birth cohorts studied. Mayer and Wagner (1986) did separate analyses for cohorts born around 1930, 1940 and 1950, and found that for some determinants the impact on the process of leaving home declines across the cohorts. Blom (1994) and Manting (1994) found that some factors weaken across cohorts for behaviour that becomes more standard over time (cohabitation) and increase in importance for options becoming less standard over time or for new options (marriage without prior cohabitation). For women born between 1945 and 1959 De Jong Gierveld and Liefbroer (1992) showed that the impact of educational attainment weakens with respect to entry into cohabitation. Manting (1994) argued that factors may change across cohorts because the behaviour under study might change in meaning over time. She expected that, as a result of individualisation and secularisation, factors from the family background or past life history would weaken across cohorts for behaviour that becomes more standard over time, and might gain in strength across cohorts for behaviour that becomes more unusual over time. This argument might also be apparent in the process of leaving home, since leaving home to marry has become less standard over time and leaving home to cohabit or to live alone has become more standard, especially in the Netherlands (Mulder & Manting, 1994). Therefore, the expectation in this study is that, across the birth cohorts, the effect of parental resources on leaving the parental home increases for those who leave to marry and declines for those who leave to cohabit or to live without a partner.

Circumstances change as people grow older. Life course theory postulates that circumstances may affect persons early in life differently, compared to later in life. Manting (1994) expected that with increasing age, individuals would become more socially, psychologically and economically independent from their parents, so that parental influence on the life cycle declines. Current daily life experiences then become more important than previous life experiences. Several studies have shown that determinants have age-specific influences. De Jong Gierveld et al. (1991) found that young adults whose parents attach great importance to religion are much more likely to leave the parental home to start living with a partner than young adults whose parents attach relatively little importance to religion. This effect, however, is only apparent among young adults in their teens and disappears among young adults aged 20 and over. With regard to entry into cohabitation or marriage, Manting (1994) found a declining effect of previous life determinants with age. Axinn and Thornton (1992) also found this declining effect of parental education on the children's entry into marriage with age. The expectation in this study will also be that, with increasing age, the influence of parental resources on leaving the parental home declines for all destinations.

Over the past few decades, demographic behaviour has changed in many Western European countries. Some countries can be considered fore-runners in 'new' innovative demographic behaviour, others can be regarded as lagging behind. As a consequence, there may be country-specific differences with regard to the relationship between determinants and demographic behaviour (Blossfeld et al., 1993; Liefbroer et al., 1993).
Compared to the Netherlands, Belgium is lagging behind with respect to demographic behaviour (Liefbroer et al., 1996). The authors found considerable country-specific differences between Belgium and the Netherlands with regard to the influence of the determinants on union and family formation. These differences remained after controlling for the compositional differences of factors such as parental background, religion, educational level and activity status (Liefbroer et. al., 1996). This chapter will address the question of whether or not the effects of the family background on leaving home differ between the two countries as well.

3.3 Method and data manipulation

In order to examine the simultaneous impact of different determinants on the process of leaving the parental home, a discrete multivariate log-linear non-proportional hazard model is used (Allison, 1984; Hachen, 1988; Laird & Olivier, 1981). This is also called a competing risk model, because the reasons for leaving home involve more than one destination (Hachen, 1988). The decision to leave the parental home is a consequence of other decisions. Firstly, one decides whether or not one wishes to marry and then decides to leave home as such. In this study, three competing risks (or routes) are analysed separately in order to avoid too many interactions between these routes and other determinants. At the time when people leave home by one route, they are no longer exposed to the risk of leaving home by another. Men leave home later than women and the two groups were analysed separately so that sex-specific interactions could be avoided and sex-specific age-categories could be included.

Since the expectations postulated above explicitly presuppose the presence of non-proportionality in the determinants, the log-linear non-proportional hazard rate model was used since it relaxes the assumption of proportionality and allows for easy testing of the presence of non-proportionality (for a detailed discussion, see Manting, 1994). The conditional L2 (log-likelihood ratio chi-square) test was used to check the significance of the improvement in the model's match with a level of $p<0.01$ (Hagenaars, 1990).

Analyses were carried out on individual data taken from the Belgian survey (*NEGO V*) and the Dutch survey *(OG'93)* described in the *Technical Appendix*. The dependent variable in the multivariate analyses is the monthly hazard rate for leaving the parental home (or the institutional home) for the first time in life after the age of 16. This is the rate at which parental home will be left in an infinitesimally small age interval, given that it has not yet occurred before the start of the age interval (Liefbroer, 1991). The few respondents not living in the parental (or institutional) home at the age of 16 were eliminated from the analysis. In order to make the two data sets comparable, all life histories were censored as at December 1990. Time (in months) was measured from the age of 16 until the moment the parental home was left (irrespective of reason) or up to December 1990 (if the person still lived in the parental home). All the respondents who married within three months of leaving the parental home took the path of *direct marriage*. Young adults who left home to live together with a partner and did not marry within three months started with *unmarried cohabitation*. Those who left home to live without a partner were categorised as *leaving home without a partner*. In *OG'93*, for all those who left home and who never lived independently, it is not known whether or not the event of marriage or cohabitation occurred before or at the same time as leaving home. We assume that it occurred simultaneously. A comparison with *OG'88* in which the date of leaving home was known for all respondents made clear that cohort patterns were almost the same, implying that this assumption will not really disrupt the age patterns for leaving home. In the Netherlands, almost half of respondents lived alone, whereas the other half lived with 'others'. In Belgium 61% started by living alone, living partly alone (33%) or living with 'others' (5%).
The coding and distribution of the variables used as covariates in the multivariate analyses are given in *Table 3.1*.

Table 3.1. Distribution of response on the covariates used in the analyses of leaving home in Belgium and the Netherlands (in %)

	Belgium		The Netherlands	
	men	women	men	women
route				
marriage	62	71	31	39
cohabitation	11	8	21	18
without a partner	17	15	41	40
birth cohort				
1951-55	32	30	33	33
1956-60	34	35	34	33
1961-65	34	35	33	33
church attendance of parents				
regular	49	50	52	51
irregular	24	25	15	15
none	27	25	33	35
educational level of parents				
low	57	53	53	53
medium	21	23	23	23
high	14	16	14	11
unknown	8	8	10	13
N (100%)	1813	2713	3005	3685

Sources: NEGO V 91-93 (Belgium) and OG'93 (the Netherlands).

The cohorts common to the surveys in both countries and selected for this study were born in 1951-55, 1956-60 and 1961-65. Given the trend for postponing the event of leaving home, cohorts who were relatively young at the time of the interview (born after 1965) were left out of the analysis. The analyses were performed for 4818 men and 6398 women from a combined Dutch and Belgian data set.

Different age categories were created for men and women because men leave home later than women. Considering the type of data which are common to both surveys, we restricted the parental resources to the educational level and church attendance of the parents. Since these characteristics were mostly available for both parents, theoretically there was no strong argument for neglecting the characteristics of one of the parents. Since these two characteristics are highly correlated and in order to avoid too many zeroes in the matrices, a composite variable encompassing a characteristic of the parental home was constructed. The frequency distribution of the level of parental education suggested a separate category for respondents both of whose parents had little education. In the other two categories, at least one parent had a medium or high level of education. A non-negligible remainder category consisted of parents with unknown or specific levels of education. Although parents' religious affiliation and frequency of church attendance during their childhood years (before the age of 16) can change over time, it can be regarded as a good representation of the religiousness of the parental home during upbringing. Three categories of church attendance were distinguished: a parental home where both parents attended church regularly; a parental home where either one parent attended church regularly or where both parents attended church on an irregular basis; all other combinations were placed in a third category in which there is a weak relationship with a religion or church or no relationship at all.

3.4 Patterns of leaving home: results

Before discussing the findings of the multivariate models, a description of the global trends in leaving home in the Netherlands and Belgium will be presented.
Women leave the parental home earlier than men (*Figure 3.1*). In both countries a postponement of the timing of leaving home can be discerned across these cohorts, especially for the youngest male cohort. The general process of leaving home is much faster in the Netherlands than in Belgium, both for men and women. In the youngest cohort, for example, 55% of Dutch women and 31% of Dutch men have left the parental home by the age of 20, compared to about 33% of Belgian women and 12% of Belgian men.

Besides the strong country-specific differences in the age at which young adults leave home, the kind of living arrangement they choose is quite different in both countries. Belgium lags behind in that, here, it is still much more common to leave home and marry. Even for the youngest cohort, the majority of Belgian young adults leave home to marry. Both in Belgium and the Netherlands, albeit at a different rate, the postponement of leaving home in general coincides with the postponement of leaving home to marry (*Figure 3.2*). The proportion of young adults leaving home to marry before the age of 25 in Belgium is about 20% and in the Netherlands about 27%.

Figure 3.1a. Timing of leaving the parental home for men in Belgium and the Netherlands for the cohorts 1951-55, 1956-60, 1961-65

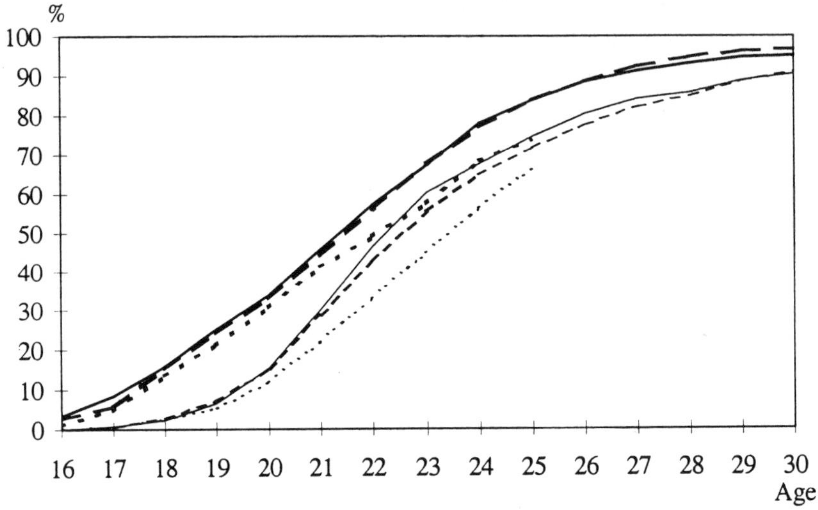

Figure 3.1b.Timing of leaving the parental home for women in Belgium and the Netherlands for the cohorts 1951-55, 1956-60, 1961-65

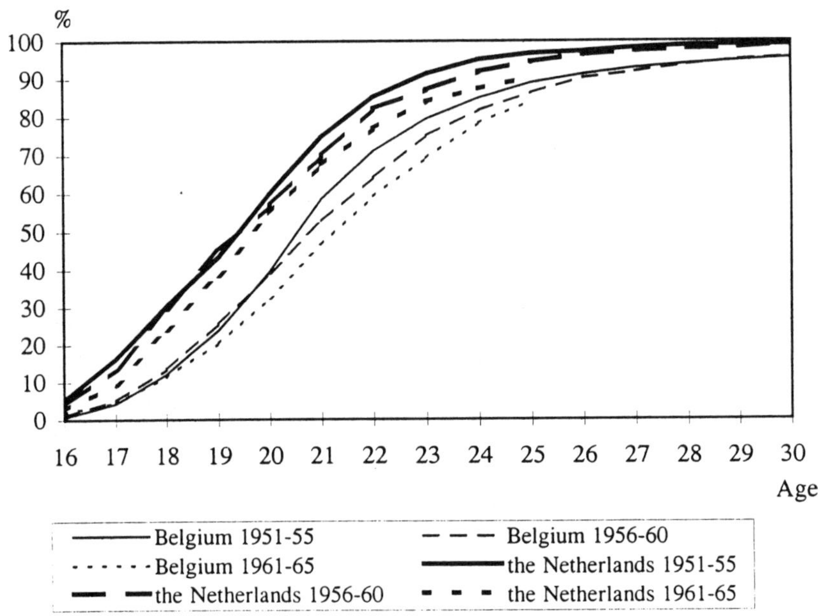

The decision to leave home to cohabit is being made at a younger age and has increased in popularity (*Figure 3.3*). The level and the rate of the increase, however, is very different in the two countries. In the Netherlands, the increase is no longer visible for the youngest male cohort whereas in Belgium the popularity of unmarried cohabitation for the youngest cohort increased to such an extent that this cohort is catching up with the oldest Dutch cohort.

In the Netherlands, leaving home followed by living without a partner did not gain much in popularity across the cohorts. In Belgium, the popularity of this route is gradually growing, but it remains at a much lower level than in the Netherlands.

Table 3.2 presents the significant interactions of the multivariate models studied.

Table 3.2. Match characteristics including main effects and significant higher-order interaction effects, for the three routes for leaving home, by sex

	Women	Men
Leaving home to marry	(CB, CA, BA, AR, AE) L2=246 df=186	(CB, CC, BA, AR, AE) L2=236 df=184
Leaving home to cohabit	(CB, CA, CR, BA) L2=247 df=197	(CB, CA, R) L2=286 df=201
Leaving home to live without a partner	(CB, CA, CR, CBE) L2=250 df=183	(CA, CR, CE) L2=237 df=197

L2=log likelihood, df=degree of freedom, C=Country, B=Birth cohort, A=age, R=Parental religion, E=Parental education.

Figure 3.2a. Leaving the parental home to marry for men in Belgium and the Netherlands for the cohorts 1951-55, 1956-60, 1961-65

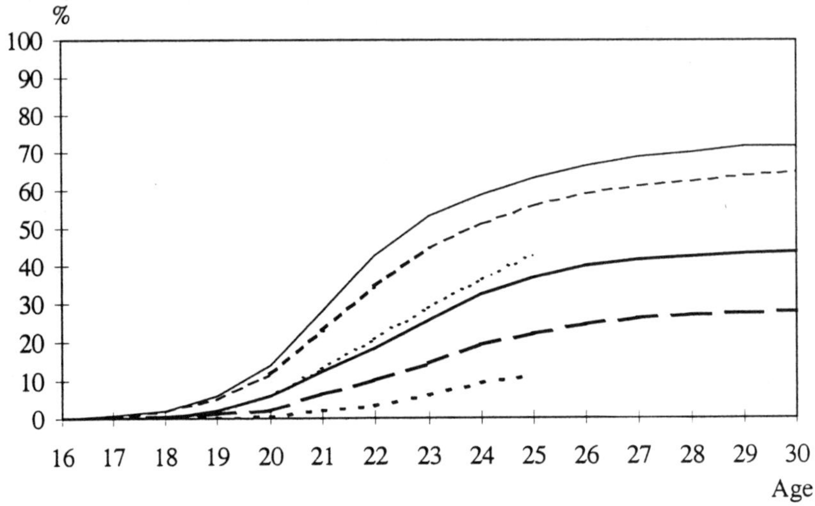

Figure 3.2b. Leaving the parental home to marry for women in Belgium and the Netherlands for the cohorts 1951-55, 1956-60, 1961-65

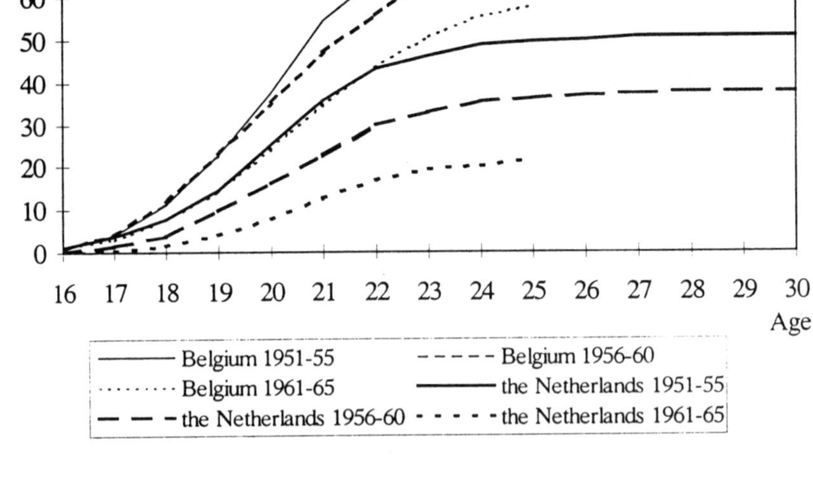

Figure 3.3a. Leaving the parental home to cohabit for men in Belgium and the Netherlands for the cohorts 1951-55, 1956-60, 1961-65

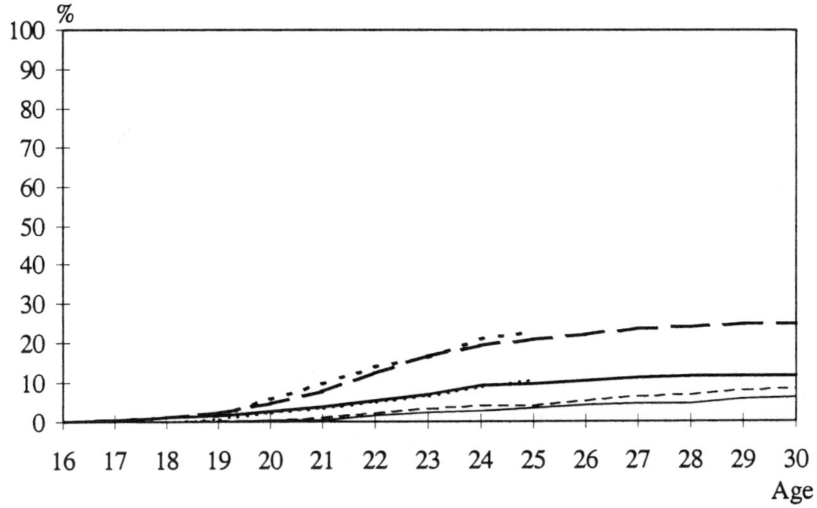

Figure 3.3b. Leaving the parental home to cohabit for women in Belgium and the Netherlands for the cohorts 1951-55, 1956-60, 1961-65

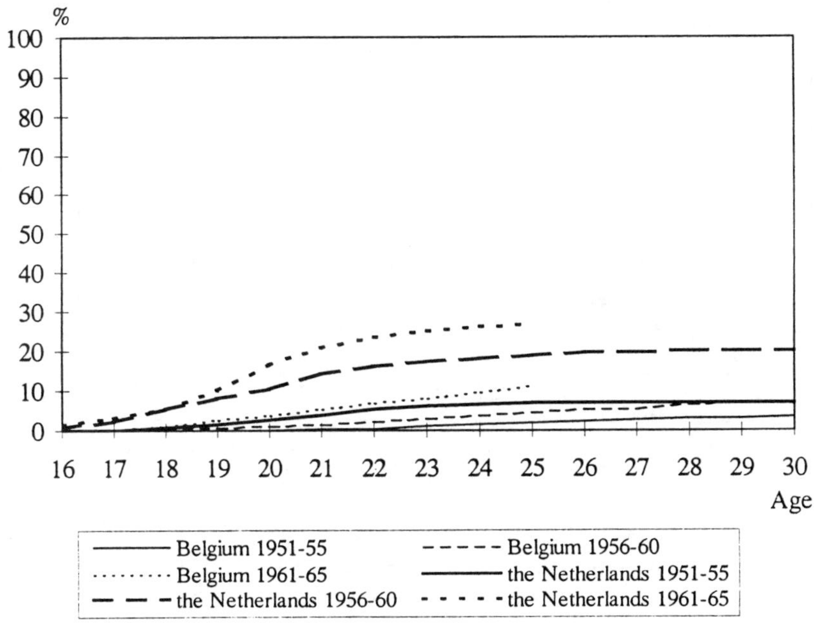

Figure 3.4a. Leaving the parental home without a partner for men in Belgium and the Netherlands for the cohorts 1951-55, 1956-60, 1961-65

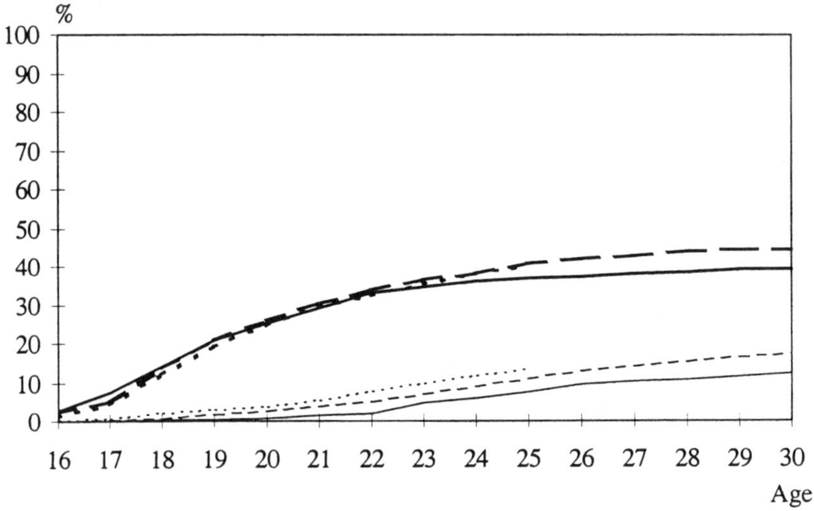

Figure 3.4b. Leaving the parental home without a partner for women in Belgium and the Netherlands for the cohorts 1951-55, 1956-60, 1961-65

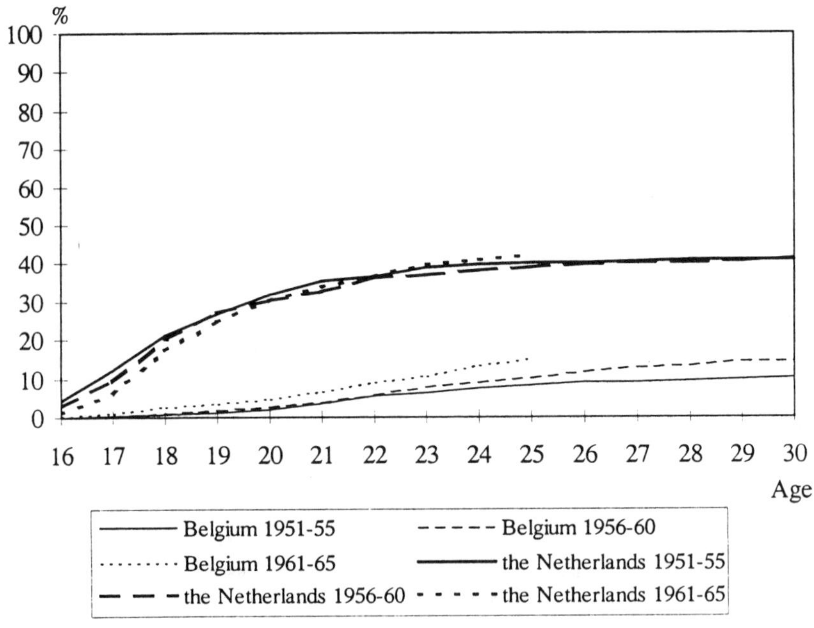

The multivariate analyses for selecting significant interactions first examine whether or not the chosen determinants - country, age and birth cohort and the two parental resources factors - have a significant impact on (one of) the routes out of the parental home. All the determinants do indeed have a significant impact, although not for all transitions. The large number of significant interactions with the country determinant make it clear that determinants differ significantly in impact on the timing of leaving home between Belgium and the Netherlands. They reveal that the different age and cohort patterns observed in the graphs are indeed significant, even after controlling for the two background factors. If the hypothesis reveals as correct that the impact of determinants is cohort-specific, then the interactions between the determinants and the birth cohort factor should lead to a significant improvement in the match of the model. Only the impact of parental education changes across the cohorts and then only for leaving home to marry. A few determinants change their meaning with the individual's age, given the significant interactions with age. Finally, the examination of whether or not the influence of determinants changes differently over the life course or across the birth cohorts for the two countries involved was supported by only one three-order interaction for the process of leaving home without a partner.

Table 3.3 presents the relative risks of leaving home to marry, to cohabit or to live without a partner for the two countries and sexes separately.
These risks are calculated from parameter estimates of the models including all the significant interaction effects shown in *Table 3.2* (these parameter estimates are not given here but can be supplied on request). A relative risk of > 1 for a certain category means that persons belonging to that category have a higher than average risk of leaving home. A relative risk of < 1 refers to a lower than average risk. The ratio is the relative risk of a certain category in Belgium divided by the relative risk of the same category in the Netherlands.

The first observation from *Table 3.3* is that the results for men and women are remarkably similar. With the exception of the influence of parental education on leaving home to cohabit, all the determinants have a similar positive or negative influence for men and for women on the processes of leaving home, only the level varies (*Table 3.3*). Belgian men and women both have a higher risk of leaving home to marry and a much lower risk of flying the nest to cohabit or live alone than young Dutch adults (consistent with the trends shown in *Figures 3.2, 3.3 and 3.4*).

Table 3.3. Relative risks of leaving home to marry, to cohabit or to live without a partner, for women and men. Belgium and the Netherlands

		women			men		
		Belgium	the Netherlands	Ratio[1]	Belgium	the Netherlands	Ratio[1]
		relative risk of home-leaving and marry					
Birth cohort	1951-55	1.24	1.34	0.93	1.42	1.24	1.14
	1956-60	1.12	0.93	1.21	1.43	0.90	1.58
	1961-65	1.04	0.56	1.87	1.10	0.40	2.78
Age	female:16-20; male:16-21	0.64	0.30	2.11	0.56	0.17	3.33
	female:21-23; male:22-25	1.99	1.63	1.22	2.77	1.64	1.68
	female:24+; male:26+	1.14	1.40	0.81	1.44	1.61	0.90
Parental church frequency	high	1.22	0.95	1.28	1.49	0.87	1.71
	intermediate	1.21	0.94	1.28	1.25	0.73	1.71
	other	0.98	0.77	1.28	1.21	0.70	1.71
Parental education	both low	1.56	1.22	1.28	1.78	1.04	1.71
	at least one medium	1.09	0.85	1.28	1.36	0.80	1.71
	at least one high	0.70	0.54	1.28	0.80	0.46	1.71
	other	1.39	1.08	1.28	1.52	0.89	1.71

Table 3.3. (continued) Relative risks of leaving home to marry, to cohabit or to live without a partner, for women and men. Belgium and the Netherlands

		women			men		
		Belgium	the Netherlands	Ratio[1]	Belgium	the Netherlands	Ratio[1]
		relative risk of home-leaving and cohabit					
Birth cohort	1951-55	0.28	1.08	0.26	0.39	1.06	0.37
	1956-60	0.47	2.53	0.19	0.54	2.21	0.25
	1961-65	1.07	2.60	0.41	0.99	2.00	0.50
Age	female:16-20; male:16-21	0.11	0.85	0.13	0.11	0.55	0.19
	female:21-23; male:22-25	0.63	3.29	0.19	0.91	2.90	0.31
	female:24+; male:26+	2.04	2.54	0.80	2.21	2.94	0.75
Parental church frequency	high	0.18	1.13	0.16	0.37	1.03	0.36
	intermediate	0.72	2.39	0.30	0.64	1.81	0.36
	other	1.11	2.64	0.42	0.90	2.53	0.36
Parental education		--	--	--	--	--	--

Table 3.3. (continued) Relative risks of leaving home to marry, to cohabit or to live without a partner, for women and men. Belgium and the Netherlands

		women			men		
		Belgium	the Netherlands	Ratio[1]	Belgium	the Netherlands	Ratio[1]
		relative risk of home-leaving and living without a partner					
Cohort	1951-55	0.36	1.91	0.19	--	--	--
	1956-60	0.60	1.93	0.31			
	1961-65	0.70	1.81	0.39			
Age	female:16-20;male:16-21	0.14	1.51	0.09	0.16	0.73	0.22
	female:21-23;male:22-25	0.68	2.04	0.33	0.84	1.84	0.46
	female:24+;male:26+	1.62	2.16	0.75	1.82	3.01	0.60
Parental church frequency	high	0.48	2.08	0.23	0.62	1.60	0.39
	intermediate	0.47	1.71	0.28	0.51	1.50	0.34
	other	0.66	1.88	0.35	0.78	1.69	0.46
Parental education	both low	0.43	1.24	0.35	0.34	0.94	0.36
	at least one medium	0.61	2.08	0.29	0.79	1.89	0.42
	at least one high	0.78	3.26	0.24	0.88	2.75	0.32
	other	0.39	1.49	0.26	0.66	1.33	0.50

[1] Relative risk of Belgium divided by relative risk of the Netherlands

Source: NEGO V 91 (Belgium) and OG'93 (the Netherlands)

Since the decline in marriage risk is much higher in the Netherlands than in Belgium across the cohorts, it becomes clear that the later one is born, the larger the difference in marriage risk between Belgium and the Netherlands. Belgian women born in 1951-55 had a 0.9 times lower risk of leaving home through marriage than Dutch women born in the same years. For women born in the period 1961-65, Belgian women had a 1.9 times higher risk than Dutch women. The same pattern is also visible for men (1.1 and 2.8 respectively).
Country-specific differences in leaving home to cohabit were at a maximum for the 1956-60 cohort. The youngest Belgian cohort seems to be catching up the youngest Dutch cohort. The risk of leaving home without a partner did not change much across the cohorts. Only for women in Belgium did it increase. Yet, the risk of leaving home without a partner is still 2.6 times higher in the Netherlands than in Belgium for the youngest female cohort. Country-specific differences are absent for men.

The risks of leaving home fluctuate strongly with age. In general, the relative risks of marriage are highest in the middle age category, whereas those of leaving home for more modern living arrangements rise linearly with age, except for the cohabitation route for Dutch women. For all the processes concerned, differences between Belgium and the Netherlands become smaller as age increases. Young Belgians have a higher marriage risk when they are young, but young Dutch adults catch up when they are older. The Dutch have a strong lead when they are younger with regard to the more modern routes, but a smaller one when they are older.

Regular church attendance by parents moderately stimulates the process of leaving the parental home via marriage and strongly slows down the process of leaving home by cohabitation. People whose parents both went to church frequently during childhood have a higher risk of marriage and a much lower risk of cohabitation than other people. The effect of parental religion is less systematic for leaving without a partner.
Parental religion does not have a country-specific influence on leaving home via marriage. The fact that people from very religious families have a higher risk of marriage in Belgium than in the Netherlands stems from the overall higher risk of marriage (1.28 for women and 1.71 for men) in Belgium than in the Netherlands. With regard to the process of leaving home via cohabitation, however, regular church attendance by parents is much more important in Belgium than in the Netherlands, at least for women. For the less traditional routes differences between the countries are stronger for women than for men.

As expected, higher parental education reduces the risk of leaving home through marriage and increases the risks of leaving home without a partner. The effect of parental education on leaving home without a partner is most pronounced for parents with a high educational level.
Surprisingly, parents' educational attainment does not have any significant impact on leaving home to cohabit. The effect of parental education on leaving home through marriage is similar for both countries. Although Belgium can be considered culturally a more traditional country than the Netherlands, leading us to expect a different relationship between parental resources and leaving home, the impact of the intellectual climate in the parental home does not work in a country-specific way.

Table 3.4. Changing significance of parents' education on leaving home to live without a partner, by birth cohort and country

	Belgium			The Netherlands		
Birth cohort	1951-55	1956-60	1961-65	1951-55	1956-60	1961-65
Parental education						
Low versus medium	0.57	0.64	0.94	0.60	0.60	0.58
Low versus high	0.60	0.46	0.60	0.48	0.33	0.34
Medium versus high	0.88	0.71	0.63	0.80	0.55	0.59

Source: NEGO V 91-93 (Belgium) and OG'93 (the Netherlands)

With regard to the changing links between the determinants and the different processes of leaving home across the cohorts, only the effect of parental education on the process of leaving home to live without partner is birth cohort-specific (*Table 3.4*). Moreover, these changes are only in accordance with the expectations for Belgian women, in that the differences between a parental home with a low and a medium educational level and between a low and a high level disappears across the cohorts. The differences between those with a medium and a high level, however, increase across the cohorts. Young adults who lived in a parental home with poorly educated parents have caught up in terms of leaving home to live without a partner. Young adults who have highly educated parents have built up a strong lead for this route. In the Netherlands the cohort fluctuations are smaller.

Table 3.5. Changing significance of certain determinants across the life cycle for leaving home and marrying/cohabitation

		age					
		women			men		
Leaving home via marriage		16-20	21-23	24+	16-21	22-25	26+
Birth cohort	1956-60 versus 1951-55	0.80	0.71	0.87	0.69	0.77	1.17
	1961-65 versus 1951-55	0.45	0.53	0.85	0.32	0.47	0.83
Parental church attendance	intermediate versus high	1.32	0.86	0.85	1.19	0.90	0.55
	other versus high	1.35	0.70	0.56	1.11	0.76	0.63
Parental education	medium versus low	0.53	0.63	1.01	0.60	0.84	0.91
	high versus low	0.24	0.42	0.87	0.21	0.43	1.01

		women		
Leaving home via cohabitation		16-20	21-23	24+
Birth co-hort	1956-60 versus 1951-55	3.41	1.81	1.29
	1961-65 versus 1951-55	4.92	3.37	1.70

The idea that parental determinants change in impact with age is only visible in the process of leaving home to marry. Also, there are age-specific cohort patterns in the process of leaving home to cohabit (*Table 3.5*). The postponement of marriage is highest when young and is lower when one is older. From the interaction between parental religion and age, one learns that the higher risk for marriage in less religious parental homes when young, turns into a lower risk of marriage when older. In highly religious families, marriage is postponed when younger but later. The changing impact of parental education with age for the marriage risks corresponds to the hypothesis. The educational characteristics of the parental home no longer have an impact on the marriage behaviour of the children as they marry later.

With regard to the cohabitation route, it becomes clear that the differences between the three cohorts are wide when they are younger but disappear later. The oldest cohort was very reluctant to leave the parental home through cohabitation while young.

3.5 Summary and conclusions

There are many differences in the timing and patterns of leaving home between Belgium and the Netherlands. Firstly, young Belgians leave home later than young Dutch adults. Secondly, Belgium can be regarded as lagging behind the Netherlands in that young Belgian adults (still) leave home much more often via the traditional pattern than the Dutch.
Even the majority of Belgians born in the first half of the nineteen-sixties leave home to marry. In the Netherlands, it is much more common to leave home for the less traditional destinations of cohabitation and living without an intimate partner.

The fact that Belgian people are older when they leave home stems from the fact that the majority leave home only to marry. Thus, the 'old' situation where fluctuations in marriage are the primary explanation for fluctuations in flying the nest still holds true for Belgium. In the Netherlands, however, fluctuations in leaving home result simultaneously from fluctuations in marriage, cohabitation and living without a partner.
An explanation for the Belgian delay might be that, for Belgians, it is rather unusual to leave home without an income of one's own. Even young people with a student grant or unemployment benefit remain at home until they have a job and thus their own income. In the Netherlands, however, many students leave home irrespective of whether or not they have a state grant and/or are financially dependent on their parents.
According to Liefbroer et al. (1996), the higher level of state grants as well as the higher level of unemployment benefits in the Netherlands might be one of the causes for Dutch young adults being more likely to start a partnership or a family. It might also be a cause of their earlier exit from home to cohabit or to live without a partner. No evidence was found for the assumption that compositional differences in the determinants of the process under study might influence country-specific differences. The composition with respect to education and church attendance among the respondents' parents is similar for both countries and differences between Belgium and the Netherlands in leaving home are almost completely unaffected by compositional differences in these two determinants.

Despite a similar composition, the links between these parental resources and leaving home differ for Belgium and the Netherlands. Although in both countries the less traditional ways of leaving home are the least popular among children from religious parents and the most popular among children whose parents do not go to church, the differences between these subgroups are much larger in Belgium (only for women) than in the Netherlands. This might be caused by the further diffusion of these new options in the Netherlands. When cohabitation started to emerge in the Netherlands, it was only chosen by a selective part of the population. In the nineteen-seventies, this option was popular among highly educated, non-religious individuals living in large cities (De Feijter, 1991; De Jong Gierveld & Liefbroer, 1992; Manting, 1994). By the mid-1980s, when cohabitation had become common practice and a highly accepted way of living, it was also a choice (although still at a lower level) made by less well-educated, religious people, living in smaller cities (De Feijter, 1991). In Belgium, however, the diffusion has not (yet) gone that far. If Belgium follows a diffusion pattern similar to that of the Netherlands in the future, the influence of parental religion on leaving home via less traditional pathways will weaken in due course.

Country-specific differentials according to the parents' religion are absent in the case of flying the nest to marry. Both in the Netherlands and in Belgium, leaving home to marry is most popular among those with a highly religious background, but differences are not that pronounced.

Country-specific differentiation is not that obvious with respect to parental education: it is only present in its effect on leaving home to live without a partner. The differentiation in the likelihood to do so is much larger in the Netherlands than in Belgium. This might be considered as follows. Many young Dutch people leave home to live alone when they go to university or college outside their home town. The educational aspirations of highly educated parents seem to go along with children leaving their parental home earlier in order to study. In Belgium, however, the fulfilment of parents' educational aspirations for their children does not coincide with full-time nest-flying. Belgian students participating in higher education leave home only for weekdays, but go back home at weekends.

One unexpected finding is that the parents' education does not affect the transition from home to cohabitation at all, nor are there country-specific differentials.

In Belgium and the Netherlands, women leave home earlier than men. This is quite common. Despite this difference, determinants influence men and women leaving home in almost exactly the same way. One of the expectations is that the popularity of leaving home without an intimate partner increases across Belgian female birth cohorts but remains constant among Belgian male birth cohorts. Belgian women are thus pioneers compared to Belgian men.
Another difference between men and women is the impact of parental education. This only changes in significance across female cohorts for leaving home to live without a partner. This determinant changes in significance across cohorts. Cohort changes in the influence of determinants were expected because the routes under study changed in significance over time. In addition, although the impact of parental education does change in significance across the cohorts, it changes in the expected direction only in the case of Belgium.

A declining influence of parental resources with increasing age was thought to be present because, as they grow older, children encounter life situations outside the home, experience changes in their own individual life domains, earn their own income, find a steady partner and increasingly make decisions independently of their parents. The impact of parents declines with age only with respect to leaving home to marry. The lack of support for this from the results for the two less traditional routes may be due to the fact that changes in these life domains occur after one has left home to cohabit or to live without a steady partner, not before. As such, parents still exert an important influence on their children's behaviour when they are at home, whatever their age. Perhaps this does not hold true for those who marry, as they will generally have finished their education and have their own income. As a consequence, the influence of parents on children who leave home to marry later is smaller due to the increasing importance of the individual's own experiences in other individual life domains.

The process of leaving home is undergoing rapid change, especially in the Netherlands. It is no longer appropriate to focus on marriage fluctuations as the sole explanation for fluctuations in leaving home. Moreover, distinguishing between the type of union chosen at the time of leaving home facilitates a deeper understanding of the process of flying the nest, since links between underlying forces and leaving home differ for entry into marriage or cohabitation at the time of leaving home.

References

Allison, P.D. (1984), *Event history analysis. Regression for longitudinal event data*, Beverly Hills: Sage, Sage University Paper Series on Quantitative Applications in the Social Science.

Axinn, W.G., A. Thornton (1992), The influence of parental resources and the timing of the transition to marriage. *Social Science Research*, 21, pp. 261-285.

Baanders, A., Th. van Leeuwen, M. Ploegmakers (1989), *Uit huis gaan van jongeren*. The Hague: Ministerie van Volkshuisvesting, Ruimtelijke Ordening en Milieubeheer.

Blom, S. (1994), Marriage and cohabitation in a changing society: experience of Norwegian men and women born in 1945 and 1960. *European Journal of Population*, 9, pp. 143-173.

Blossfeld, H.P., A. De Rose, J.M. Hoem and G. Röhwer (1993), *Education, modernization and the risk of marriage disruption: differences in the effect of women's educational attainment in Sweden, West Germany and Italy*. Stockholm Research Reports in Demography, 76.

Corijn, M. (1993), Leefvormen van jongvolwassenen in Vlaanderen. pp. 36-53. In: M. du Bois-Reymond and J. de Jong Gierveld (eds.), *Volwassen worden. Generaties toen en nu: transities in de levensloop*. Bohn: Stafleu Van Loghum.

Corijn, M. (1995). Determinanten van de leefvorm en van de aanvang van de gezinsvorming in Vlaanderen. Resultaten van het NEGO V-onderzoek In: *Gezinstypes en intergenerationele netwerken*. Verslagboek tweede Vlaamse Gezinsconferentie. Brussels.

De Feijter, H. (1991), *Voorlopers bij demografische veranderingen*, NIDI, report no. 22, The Hague.

De Jong Gierveld, J., A.C. Liefbroer and E. Beekink (1991), The effect of parental resources on patterns of leaving home among young adults in the Netherlands. *European Sociological Review*, 7, pp. 55-71.

De Jong Gierveld, J. and A.C. Liefbroer (1992), Een verkenning van de invloed van veranderingen in opleidingsdeelname en arbeidsparticipatie op het demografisch gedrag van vrouwen 1-17. In: H.J. Bronsema, R.F. van der Erf (eds.). *Emancipatie en bevolkingsontwikkeling: Hechte partners?* The Hague: Nederlandse Vereniging voor Demografie.

Goldscheider, F.K. and J. Da Vanzo (1989), Pathways to independent living in early adulthood: marriage, semi-autonomy, and premarital residential independence. *Demography*, 26, pp. 597-613.

Goldscheider, F.K. and L.J. Waite (1987), Nest-leaving patterns and the transition to marriage for young men and women. *Journal of Marriage and the Family*, 49, 507-516.

Hachen, D. S. (1988), The competing risk model: A method for analyzing processes with multiple types of events. *Sociological Methods and Research*, 17, pp. 21-54.

Hagenaars, J.A. (1990), *Categorical longitudinal data. Log-linear panel, trend and cohort analysis*. London: Sage Publications.

Laird, N. and D. Olivier (1981), Covariance analysis of censored survival data using log-linear analysis techniques. *Journal of the American Statistical Association*, 76, pp. 231-240.

Latten, J.J. (1990), Jongeren bleven in jaren '80 weer langer bij hun ouders wonen. Ontwikkeling sinds de jaren '60, *Maandstatistiek Bevolking, CBS,* 10, pp. 14-24.

Lesthaeghe, R. and G. Moors (1992), De gezinsrelaties: De ontwikkeling en stabilisatie van patronen pp. 19-68. In: J. Kerkhofs et al. (eds.), *De versnelde ommekeer.* Tielt: Lannoo.

Liefbroer, A.C. (1991), *Kiezen tussen ongehuwd samenwonen en trouwen. Een onderzoek naar plannen en gedrag van jong-volwassenen omtrent relatievorming.* Amsterdam: Centrale Huisdrukkerij Vrije Universiteit.

Liefbroer, A.C., M. Corijn and J. De Jong Gierveld (1996), *Similarity and diversity in the onset of family formation in the Low Countries.* Brussels: CBGS Document 3.

Manting, D. (1994), *Dynamics in marriage and cohabitation.* An intertemporal, life course analysis of first union formation and dissolution. Amsterdam: Thesis publishers/PDOD.

Mayer, K.U. and N.B. Tuma (1990). Life course Research and Event History Analysis: An overview. pp. 3-20. In: Mayer, K.U. and N.B. Tuma (eds.). *Event History Analysis in Life Course research*, The University of Wisconsin Press.

Mayer, K.U. and M. Wagner (1986), Wann verlassen Kinder das Elternhaus? pp. 17-33. In: A. Herlth and K.P. Strohmeier (eds.) *Lebenslauf und Familienentwicklung. Mikroanalyses des Wandels familialer Lebensformen.* Opladen: Leske+Budrich.

Mulder, C.H. (1993), *Migration dynamics: a life course approach,* Amsterdam: Thesis publishers/PDOD.

Mulder, C.H. and P. Hooimeijer (1995), Alleen of met een partner uit huis: de dynamiek in twee processen. *STEPRO Working Document.* Utrecht: Faculteit Ruimtelijke Wetenschappen.

Mulder, C.H. and D, Manting (1994), Strategies of nest-leavers: settling down versus flexibility. *European Sociological Review*, 10, pp. 155-172.

Runyan, W.M. (1984), The Life Course as a Theoretical Orientation. pp. 81-99. In: W.M. Runyan (ed.), *Life Histories and Psychobiography. Explorations in theory and method.* New York: Oxford.

Ryder, N. B. (1965), The cohort as a concept in the study of social change. *American Sociological Review*, 30, pp. 843-861.

Visser, H. (1994), Kinderen worden volwassen. *Maandstatistiek Bevolking*, CBS, June, pp. 9-17.

Wagner, M. and J. Huinink (1991), Neuere Trends beim Auszug aus dem Elternhaus. pp. 39-62. In: G. Buttler, H.J. Hoffmann-Nowotny and G. Schmitt-Rink (Hrsg.), *Acta Demographica.* Heidelberg: Physica-Verlag.

Weick, S. (1992), Determinanten des Auszugs aus der elterlichen Wohnung 86-107. In: A. Diekmann, S. Weick (Hrsg.), *Der Familienzyklus als sozialer Process.* Berlin: Duncker & Humblot.

4. FERTILITY

Andries de Jong and Edith Lodewijckx

4.1 Introduction

This chapter aims to explain differences in fertility levels in Belgium and the Netherlands by relating them to demographic and socio-cultural factors. The level of fertility for women born between 1951 and 1970 is examined on the basis of data from fertility surveys held in both countries in the early 1990s. Young cohorts of women were at the beginning or in the middle of the process of childbearing at the time the surveys were held, while the older cohorts had almost completed their family. This means that the analysis of actual fertility primarily gives an indication of differences in the tempo of family formation. In order to gain an impression of differences in completed fertility, an analysis has also been made of the level of fertility women expect to have by the end of their fertile period.
The fertility of all women will be examined in the analysis, as well as the composition by birth order, i.e. childlessness and the number of children per mother. The decision to have children at all may differ from the decision as to how many children are wanted. Since most women ultimately want to become mothers, differences in the actual childlessness of certain cohorts might primarily reflect differences in the processes of postponing and catching up on motherhood.
Once women have become mothers, the effects of background variables on the level and tempo of fertility may not be the same.

Section 4.2 gives an overview of developments in fertility in the two countries. The next section deals with the data and the method of analysis. Then the analysis itself will be given and, finally, some conclusions and a discussion will be presented.

J. de Beer and F. Deven (eds.), Diversity in Family Formation, 59–88.

4.2 Developments in fertility

Figure 4.1 shows the development of the Total Fertility Rate (TFR) in the Netherlands and Belgium since 1950. This rate represents the average number of children per woman if women were to experience no mortality and have the age-specific fertility rates (number of births related to the women of a specific age) for a specified calendar year.

Figure 4.1.Total fertility rate for the period 1950-1995, Belgium, the Netherlands

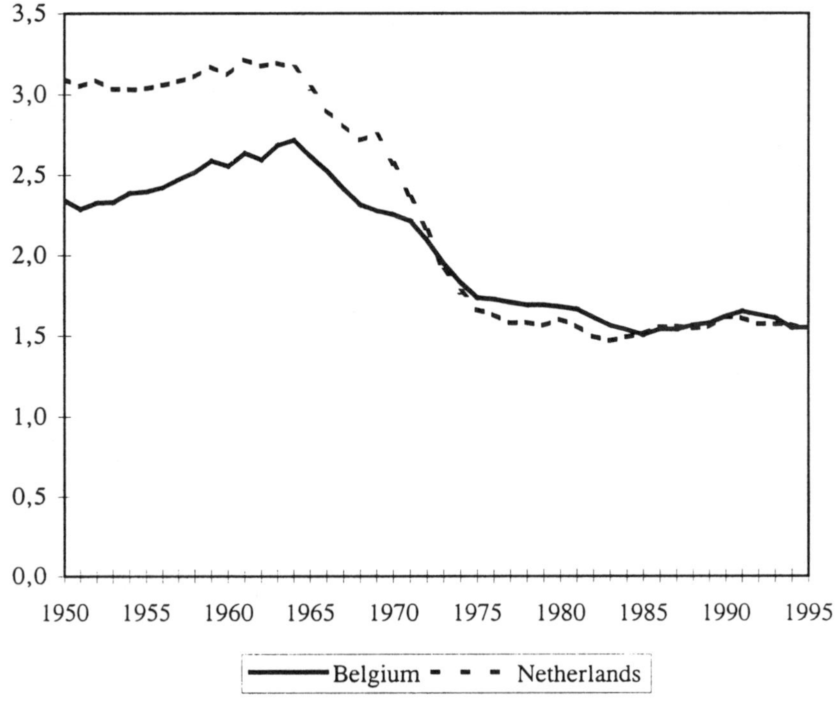

Source: Eurostat

In the 1960s the Netherlands had a much higher TFR than Belgium (about a half-child more). Following a more intense decline in the Netherlands, however, the rates became almost the same in the two countries by the early 1970s. The decline is related to the falling popularity of the large family and to the postponement of having children (De Jong, 1998). Households with two children became the most popular family size. The catching up process of postponed births may be seen as the explanation for the slight increase in the TFR in the second half of the 1980s, although this has stagnated in recent years.

The TFRs of Belgium and the Netherlands observed in the nineteen-nineties (around 1.6) are not the lowest in Europe. In Mediterranean countries and Germany, for example, this rate fluctuates around 1.3 while in Scandinavian countries, values of 1.8 are rather common.

The pattern of a considerable decline in fertility since 1965 has been seen in all modern-industrialised western countries (De Jong, 1998). In order to describe these developments, Lesthaeghe and Van de Kaa (1986) and Van de Kaa (1993) developed the concept of the *Second Demographic Transition*. The rapid social and economic changes of European societies over the past three decades can be characterised as the process of modernisation. This involves a shift from a manufacturing and goods-producing economy to a service economy. The resulting 'post-industrial' or welfare state offers opportunities for high living standards to families and individuals. Women remain in full-time education longer and participate more often in the labour market. Women face the difficult choice between 'career' and 'family'. This means that having children may lead to lost opportunities. The decision to have a first child will be made if it is likely to contribute to the self-fulfilment of the women and her partner (Van de Kaa, 1993).

Lesthaeghe and Verleye (1992) point to the sequence of socio-cultural developments. The second transition started with an increase in divorce, followed by the postponement of marriage and childbirth. Secondly, cohabitation is becoming more and more accepted, not only as a union ('paperless marriage') between men and women, but also as a framework for childbirth. In the final stage, fertility at increased ages is going to rise due to the catching-up process. Innovations start in some vanguard countries (Denmark and Sweden), from where they spread to other regions.

In a detailed study by the United Nations (1992) the fertility decline can also be explained within the context of economic development and industrialisation. The rebuilding after World War II led to the increased participation of women in the labour force. Technological progress required more skills through longer education and training. This facilitated the extension of mass education. The desire for greater participation in social life extended to the desire for increased access to fertility regulation. This encouraged the spread of contraceptive knowledge and practice. In the post-war years, new societal conditions emerged. Cultural values and social norms underwent considerable changes. There appears to be a shift in couples' 'life goals'. There is a tendency towards an increased need to satisfy more material aspirations. The importance of having additional children has diminished. Social rewards and individual satisfaction can be achieved through the woman's work outside the home and the additional income gained, providing a more fulfilling lifestyle than that achieved from rearing additional children. Hence, according to the United Nations, norms favouring smaller families became dominant.

Cruijsen (1991) speaks about the demographic consequences of the road to a more pluriform society with complete emancipation for women. Key words used to summarise these processes are 'individualism' and 'modernisation'. An increasing proportion of young European adult women cannot and will no longer live with traditional societal and family roles. This trend has been encouraged by recent developments on the labour market. During the 1980s, in most industrial countries, a sharp increase in job opportunities in the so-called service sector took place. In some countries, a significant decline in the average income of single-income households during the first half of the 1980s may more or less have forced cohabiting and married women to keep or to take a (part-time) job outside the home to maintain a certain standard of living.

Cruijsen (1991) also mentions that young generations are more materialistic and less altruistic. This opinion seems to be confirmed by the results of a European comparative survey (Moors and Palomba, 1995). In most countries, the reason often mentioned in this survey for not having children was the desire to maintain the current standard of living. Another important reason was the perceived impossibility of combining motherhood with labour participation.

Avramov et al. (1995) characterise the childbearing conditions in Belgium as family-friendly. Belgium has a generous and comprehensive family policy which includes a range of direct transfers to families with children. There is, however, a need to improve childcare and working conditions so that parents can more easily combine work with family responsibilities.

Dutch women 'blame' the birth decline on factors related to personal development and changing life-styles, increased labour force participation and the desire among men and women for independence and personal advancement (Moors, 1995). Women in particular feel that insufficient childcare facilities are an important cause of the birth decline.

Figure 4.2. Average age for giving birth for the period 1950-1995, Belgium, the Netherlands

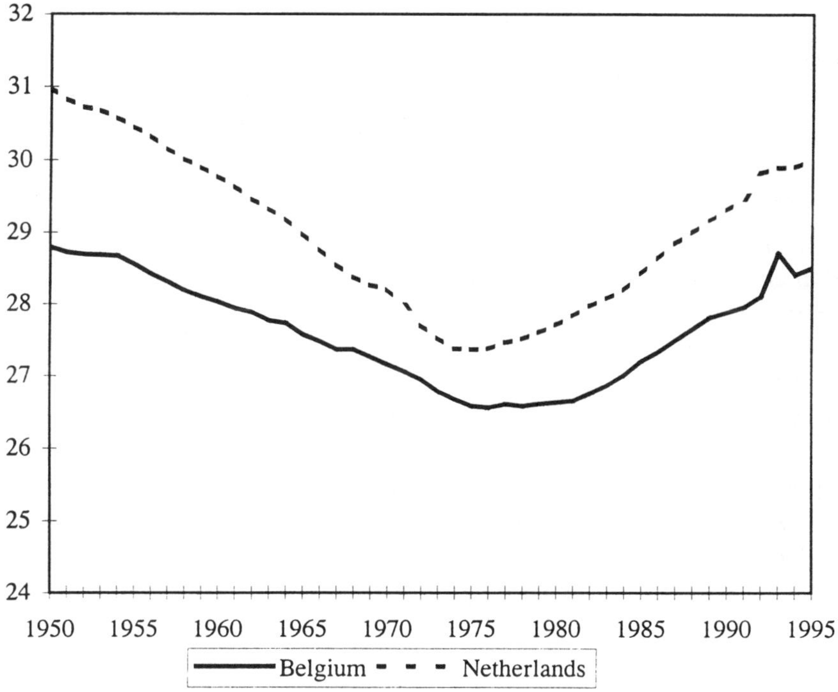

Source: Eurostat

Not only has the level of fertility changed drastically in the second half of the 20th century, but the timing of motherhood has also shown some remarkable changes. During the period 1950-1975 the average age for giving birth dropped quickly, mainly due to the reduction in births of higher orders. However, since 1975 the average age has increased. This rise is the expression of the process of postponing childbirth when younger (mainly below the age of 25) followed by catching up when older. This delay is related to socio-economic developments such as the rising level of education and higher labour participation rates for women. Increasingly, women in their early twenties are engaged in full-time education.

When older, these women want to work full-time for a number of years before having children. Around the age of 30, more highly educated women eventually tend to have children before it becomes too late, in view of their declining fecundity. As a result, the average age for becoming a mother in the Netherlands is the highest in Europe.

Trends in the Total Fertility Rate and the average age for becoming a mother may be traced back to developments in the composition of the population by background variables which have a distinctive influence on the level of fertility or rate of childbirth. The analysis by Callens and Schoenmaeckers (1993) reveals that both educational attainment and religious denomination are important variables in explaining the final number of children and the timing of first birth in Belgium. In the Netherlands, according to de Graaf (1985), both educational level and religious denomination, as well as living arrangements have a considerable effect on the expected final level of fertility. The percentage of women expecting to remain childless is higher among single women than among those who are living together. Fluctuations in the tempo of childbirth are related to the background variables of educational level, religious denomination and occupation around the first birth (De Jong, 1987). Women who worked at the beginning of the pregnancy and resumed work after their confinement had a longer first birth interval than those who had never worked or those who stopped working after the first birth. According to Van Hoorn (1991), the expected number of children is smaller for women who consider that having a job is very important compared to women who are primarily family-oriented.

4.3 Data and method

In the Dutch Fertility and Family Survey (*OG'93*) women were asked to state their number of live-born children and the additional number of children they still expected to have. Both a low and high variant could be given, i.e. the lowest and highest additional number of children a respondent expected to have. In this analysis, the low figure is added to the actual number of children in order to compute the expected number of children. Monitoring the data from previous surveys has demonstrated that even the low variant will not be fully realised in practice, so the high variant is not considered a realistic expected family size.

In the Belgian Fertility and Family Survey (*NEGO V*) the female respondents were asked to state their actual family size and the number of children (with a minimum and maximum value) they wanted to have. A number of adjustments have been made in order to arrive at a somewhat comparable concept. For infertile couples, the expected number of children was set at the actual number while for women who stated a lower parity than the actual parity, the actual number of children was used. In all other cases, the minimum number of children the respondents wanted to have was used. In the analysis, it is assumed that the computed expected number of children thus gives an indication of how many children a woman will finally have in the absence of unforeseen events.

Referring to the discussion of background variables in section 4.2, the following variables have been used in order to explain fertility differences: birth cohort of the woman, living arrangements, level of educational attainment, church attendance and having had a paid job after the first birth. For the analysis of actual fertility, the variable birth cohort of the woman is also an indicator of the age of the woman in the year of the survey. Since the two surveys were not held at the same time, the Dutch respondents were about 1.5 years older than the Belgian respondents for each specified birth cohort at the time the actual family size was stated. As can be seen from *Figure 4.2.*, the average age for giving birth is about 1.5 year higher in the Netherlands. Overall, the fertility figures per birth cohort of women are more or less comparable between the two countries.

Multiple Classification Analysis (MCA) is used, i.e. a linear regression model with categories of variables coded as dummies. The background variables can be entered directly in MCA; this does not apply to interactions between these variables (see *Technical Appendix*).

In previous decades the educational level of women has risen sharply; more highly educated women nowadays can have different characteristics and different attitudes compared to those of some decades ago. It can also be expected that the combination of birth cohort with educational level could have an effect that may differ substantially from the addition of the effect of birth cohort and education separately, which may be interpreted as some kind of age effect. If the timing of having children differs between poorly and highly educated women, this may largely explain the differences in actual fertility between poorly and highly educated women in younger cohorts (i.e. at relatively young ages). The levels of fertility could ultimately be the same. So, only in older birth cohorts (i.e. when they are older) can the effect of educational attainment on the level of fertility be examined without the interference of timing aspects. In order to model this assumption, new dummies have been created and entered into MCA which combine the two background variables.

4.4 Childlessness

Table 4.1. gives the results of the analysis of actual childlessness. The figures between brackets indicate the relationship between a background variable and the dependent variable (either eta or beta). Before correction by the MCA model, the percentages of childless women of a certain category of specific background variable can be computed by adding the effect of this category to the grand mean.

According to the results of the two surveys, of Belgian women born between 1966 and 1970, 87% were still childless in 1991 compared to 82% of Dutch women born in the same period in 1993. Looking at women from birth cohort 1951-1955, childlessness amounted to 12% for Belgian women and 16% for Dutch women. The large difference in childlessness between the two birth cohorts does of course reflect an age effect: in the first half of their twenties, women start their fertility career, while most women enter the final stage of family formation in their late thirties.

The substantial effect of living arrangements on childlessness reveals that most single women are childless (this household position also comprises heads of single-parent families), while most married women are mothers. Most cohabiting women are also childless: it is very common for couples to cohabit first and not to marry until they want to have children. Childlessness is also strongly influenced by the educational level of the woman. The difference between poorly and highly educated women amounts to about 30 percentage points. This may either be due to a timing difference or to a real difference in the proportion who never have children. We will come back to this below. Being religious is only weakly related to being childless or not.

Table 4.1. Actual childlessness (MCA), Belgium, the Netherlands. Women born 1951-1970

	Belgium			the Netherlands			
	Unadjusted deviation **(Eta)**	Adjusted deviation **(Beta)**	Number of cases	Unadjusted deviation **(Eta)**	Adjusted deviation **(Beta)**	Number of cases	
Grand mean = 0.38			3431			3687	Grand mean = 0.43
Birth cohort							Birth cohort
- 1966-1970	0.49	0.34	768	0.39	0.27	951	- 1966-1970
- 1961-1965	0.01	0.09	949	0.05	0.13	970	- 1961-1965
- 1956-1960	-0.20	-0.18	918	-0.20	-0.19	913	- 1956-1960
- 1951-1955	-0.26	-0.22	795	-0.27	-0.25	853	- 1951-1955
	(0.58)	(0.45)		(0.52)	(0.43)		
Living arrangement							Living arrangement
- single	0.44	0.28	777	0.35	0.26	904	- single
- cohabiting	0.25	0.18	306	0.35	0.24	561	- cohabiting
- married	-0.18	-0.11	2348	-0.23	-0.17	2223	- married
	(0.55)	(0.35)		(0.57)	(0.41)		
Educational level							Educational level
- low	-0.19	-0.04	921	-0.16	-0.04	1400	- low
- medium	0.00	0.00	1254	0.08	0.00	1602	- medium
- high	0.14	0.03	1256	0.15	0.07	686	- high
	(0.26)	(0.06)		(0.26)	(0.08)		
Church attendance					n.s.		Church attendance
- regular	0.00	0.01	794	-0.06	-0.02	330	- regular
- sometimes	-0.06	-0.02	1047	-0.04	0.01	418	- sometimes
- seldom or never	-0.01	0.00	947	0.00	0.00	1521	- seldom or never
- no religion	0.11	0.03	643	0.03	0.00	1418	- no religion
	(0.12)	(0.03)		(0.06)	(0.01)		

Table 4.1. (continued) Actual childlessness (MCA), Belgium, the Netherlands. Women born 1951-1970

	Belgium			the Netherlands			
	Unadjusted deviation **(Eta)**	Adjusted deviation **(Beta)**	Number of cases	Unadjusted deviation **(Eta)**	Adjusted deviation **(Beta)**	Number of cases	
Interactions: Birth cohort x Educational level							Interactions: Birth cohort x Educational level
- 1966-1970 x low	0.22	-0.17	99	0.18	-0.16	269	- 1966-1970 x low
	(0.08)	(0.06)		(0.10)	(0.09)		
- 1961-1965 x low	-0.15	-0.18	219	-0.11	-0.20	332	- 1961-1965 x low
	(0.08)	(0.10)		(0.07)	(0.13)		
- 1961-1965 x medium	-0.03	-0.12	356	0.04	-0.11	437	- 1961-1965 x medium
	(0.02)	(0.08)		(0.03)	(0.08)		
Explained variance = 48%							Explained variance = 47%

The adjusted figures according to MCA generally show smaller differences between the categories of the background variables, since connections between background variables are now removed. Thus, the effects of birth cohort and household position are somewhat smaller, but still important. When they are young, women still live alone or live together without being married, while when they are older, most women are married. Either being older or being married leads to relatively high fertility, which is corrected by MCA. After adjustment, the effect of church attendance becomes almost nil.

At first sight, the adjusted effects of educational attainment seem very small. However, if the interactions of educational level and birth cohort are also taken into account, a rather different picture emerges. An example of the computation of the percentages of childless women will be given. For poorly educated Belgian women from cohort 1966-1970, childlessness amounts to 51%. This percentage can be computed by taking the grand mean (38%), adding the effect of cohort 1966-1970 (38% + 34% = 72%), then adding the effect of low educational level (72% - 4% = 68%) and, finally, including the interaction effect (68% - 17% = 51%).

Figure 4.3 displays the relationship between childlessness on the one hand and educational level and cohort on the other hand. The women from the two older cohorts are in their thirties and a large majority are already mothers. In these cohorts, the (main) effect of educational level applies and these effects are modest: the difference between highly and poorly educated women is 7 percentage points in Belgium and 11 percentage points in the Netherlands. The two younger birth cohorts are in their twenties or early thirties and, at this stage of their life cycle, most women become mothers for the first time. In the youngest cohort, half of the poorly educated women are already mothers while of the averagely and highly educated women, 25% to 30% have given birth to a child. In the next cohort (1961-1965), the difference in fertility between poorly and highly educated women is again large, with averagely educated women in between. Also noticeable is that Dutch women are more often childless, although they were 1.5 years older when the survey was held. This is particularly the case for highly educated women, of whom 50% of the Belgian women compared to 63% of the Dutch women are childless. This illustrates the fact that family formation takes place at a higher age in the Netherlands compared to Belgium. More highly educated women in particular delay having their first child. It remains too early to tell whether highly educated women will catch up, to the extent of achieving nearly the same level of childlessness as currently seen in the two older cohorts.

Figure 4.3. Actual childlessness, by educational level and birth cohort, Belgium, the Netherlands. Women born 1951-1970

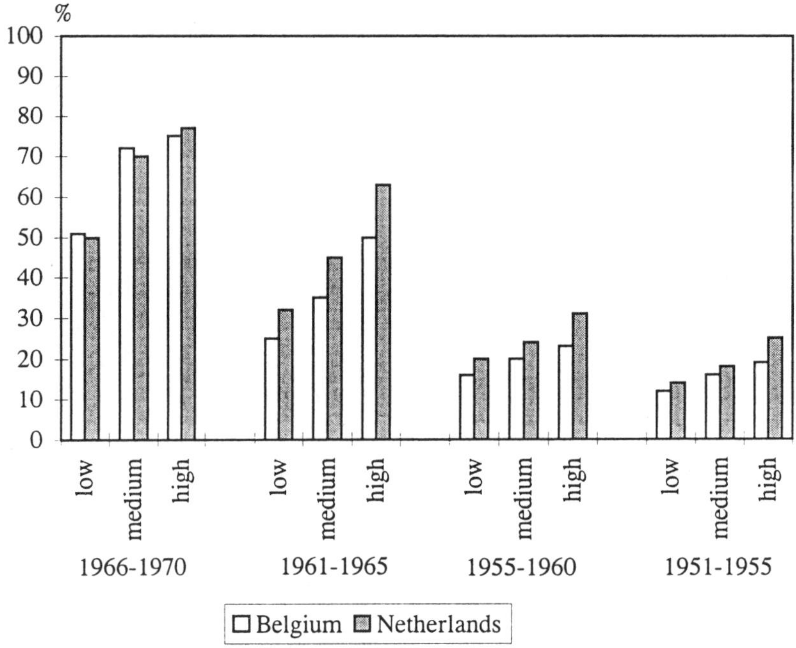

The independent variables explain nearly 50% of the total variance in the percentage of women childless at the time the survey was held, largely due to the fact that the variable birth cohort can be interpreted as an age effect. The former can not be interpreted as an age effect if the dependent variable is the expected percentage of women ultimately remaining childless. As a result, the explanatory power of MCA is drastically reduced: only 6% in Belgium and 8% in the Netherlands *(see Table 4.2.)*. It seems that the decision to stay childless ultimately has less to do with the background variables considered here, compared to the actual percentage of those childless at a certain age. This does not mean that the selected background variables have no explanatory power at all.

Unmarried couples seem more inclined not to have children. Unmarried cohabitation is largely an indication that the couple is not planning to have children in the near future. It is very common to cohabit until the couple wants to have children. Then, a large proportion will eventually marry, in order to take advantage of the legal benefits of marriage.

Table 4.2. Expected childlessness (MCA), Belgium, the Netherlands. Women born 1951-1970

	Belgium			the Netherlands			
	Unadjusted deviation **(Eta)**	Adjusted deviation **(Beta)**	Number of cases	Unadjusted deviation **(Eta)**	Adjusted deviation (Beta)	Number of cases	
Grand mean = 0.10			3431			3687	Grand mean = 0.11
Birth cohort		n.s.					Birth cohort
- 1966-1970	0.05	0.00	768	-0.02	-0.06	951	- 1966-1970
- 1961-1965	-0.01	0.00	949	-0.01	-0.01	970	- 1961-1965
- 1956-1960	-0.03	-0.01	918	0.01	0.04	913	- 1956-1960
- 1951-1955	-0.01	0.02	795	0.02	0.04	853	- 1951-1955
	(0.10)	(0.04)		(0.05)	(0.13)		
Living arrangement							Living arrangement
- single	0.10	0.10	777	0.12	0.13	904	- single
- cohabiting	0.09	0.07	306	0.02	0.03	561	- cohabiting
- married	-0.04	-0.04	2348	-0.05	-0.06	2223	- married
	(0.21)	(0.21)		(0.22)	(0.25)		
Educational level		n.s.					Educational level
- low	-0.02	0.00	921	-0.03	-0.02	1400	- low
- medium	-0.01	0.00	1254	-0.01	0.00	1602	- medium
- high	0.02	0.01	1256	0.08	0.05	686	- high
	(0.05)	(0.02)		(0.12)	(0.08)		
Church attendance							Church attendance
- regular	-0.01	-0.01	794	-0.03	-0.02	330	- regular
- sometimes	-0.03	-0.02	1047	-0.03	-0.03	418	- sometimes
- seldom or never	0.00	0.00	947	-0.03	-0.02	1521	- seldom or never
- no religion	0.07	0.05	643	0.04	0.03	1418	- no religion
	(0.12)	(0.08)		(0.11)	(0.08)		
Explained variance = 6%							Explained variance = 8%

The effect of the birth cohort of women before correction is very small in both countries and is only of some importance in the Netherlands after adjustment: in more recent cohorts, a smaller percentage of women wishes to remain childless. Educational attainment has hardly any influence on the desire to have children, especially if we look at the corrected effects of education. If we remember that the educational level did have a notable effect in cases of actual childlessness, this finding means that the effect of education on actual fertility may, in the first instance, be largely a matter of timing. More highly educated women delay having children when younger although ultimately they do want to become mothers. As a result, more highly educated women will try to catch up with the poorly educated women when they are in their thirties. The effect of church attendance is also small.

4.5 Fertility of all women

The respondents had an average of 1.2 children (Belgian women) and 1.1 children (Dutch women) at the time of the interview *(see Table 4.3.)*. In the oldest cohort, the family size is 1.8 children in both countries.

The effects of birth cohort and living arrangements are prominent, as was the case with the analysis of actual childlessness. The effect of educational level is smaller but substantial: a difference of 0.6 children (Belgian women) and 0.7 children (Dutch women) between poorly and highly educated women. Church attendance also has a considerable effect: Belgian women who attend services regularly have an average of 0.4 more children than women without a religious affiliation. This difference is even greater among Dutch women, specifically 0.55 children. This does not mean, however, that the importance of this variable is larger in the Netherlands. Those who attend church regularly or sometimes constitute 20% of the female respondents in the Netherlands, compared to 53% in Belgium. So, those who attend church services in the Netherlands constitute a specific social group with specific fertility behaviour.

Table 4.3. Actual number of children of women (MCA), Belgium, the Netherlands. Women born 1951-1970

	Belgium			the Netherlands			
	Unadjusted deviation **(Eta)**	Adjusted deviation **(Beta)**	Number of cases	Unadjusted deviation **(Eta)**	Adjusted deviation **(Beta)**	Number of cases	
Grand mean = 1.18			3431			3686	Grand mean = 1.12
Birth cohort							Birth cohort
- 1966-1970	-1.01	-0.76	768	-0.87	-0.49	951	- 1966-1970
- 1961-1965	-0.20	-0.44	949	-0.22	-0.35	969	- 1961-1965
- 1956-1960	0.48	0.51	918	0.48	0.36	913	- 1956-1960
- 1951-1955	0.66	0.67	795	0.71	0.55	853	- 1951-1955
	(0.56)	(0.52)		(0.53)	(0.38)		
Living arrangement							Living arrangement
- single	-0.86	-0.51	777	-0.73	-0.52	904	- single
- cohabiting	-0.55	-0.32	306	-0.78	-0.45	561	- cohabiting
- married	0.36	0.21	2348	0.50	0.33	2221	- married
	(0.46)	(0.27)		(0.53)	(0.35)		
Educational level							Educational level
- low	0.40	0.05	921	0.36	0.13	1399	- low
- medium	-0.08	-0.10	1254	-0.17	0.00	1602	- medium
- high	-0.22	0.06	1256	-0.33	-0.26	686	- high
	(0.22)	(0.07)		(0.25)	(0.12)		
Church attendance							Church attendance
- regular	0.12	0.10	794	0.41	0.30	330	- regular
- sometimes	0.15	0.06	1047	0.24	0.13	418	- sometimes
- seldom or never	-0.07	-0.08	947	-0.02	-0.04	1521	- seldom or never
- no religion	-0.29	-0.12	643	-0.14	-0.07	1417	- no religion
	(0.14)	(0.08)		(0.15)	(0.10)		

Table 4.3. (continued) Actual number of children of women (MCA), Belgium, the Netherlands. Women born 1951-1970

	Belgium			the Netherlands			
	Unadjusted deviation **(Eta)**	Adjusted deviation **(Beta)**	Number of cases	Unadjusted deviation **(Eta)**	Adjusted deviation **(Beta)**	Number of cases	
Interactions: Birth cohort x Educational level							Interactions: Birth cohort x Educational level
- 1966-1970 x low	-0.64	0.32	99	-0.55	-0.03	269	- 1966-1970 x low
	(0.10)	(0.05)		(0.13)	(0.01)		
- 1966-1970 x medium	-0.95	0.19	310	-0.99	-0.20	547	- 1966-1970 x medium
	(0.26)	(0.05)		(0.36)	(0.07)		
- 1961-1965 x low	0.25	0.65	219	0.12	0.26	331	- 1961-1965 x low
	(0.06)	(0.15)		(0.03)	(0.07)		
- 1961-1965 x medium	-0.19	0.39	356	-0.22	0.07	437	- 1961-1965 x medium
	(0.06)	(0.12)		(0.07)	(0.02)		
Explained variance = 40%							Explained variance = 40%

Figure 4.4. Actual number of children of women, by educational level and birth cohort, Belgium, the Netherlands. Women born 1951-1970

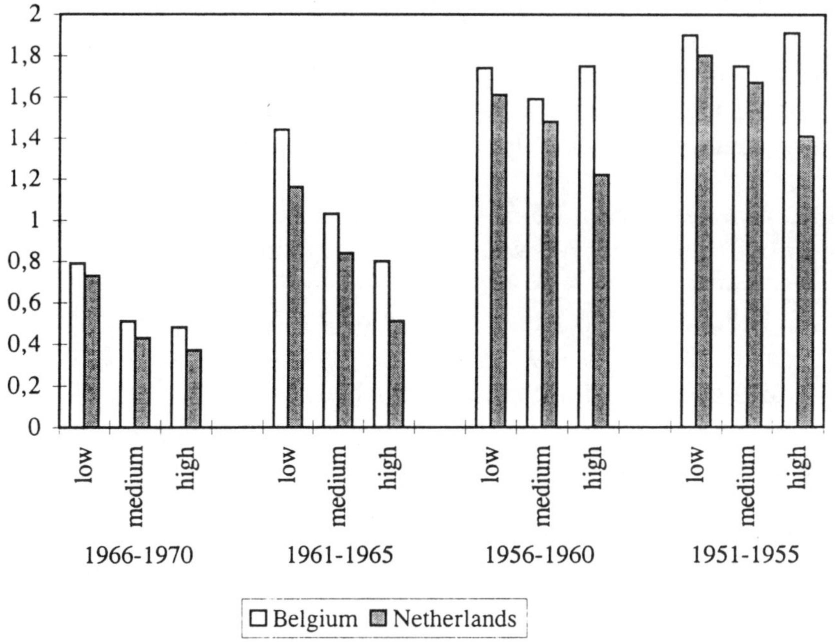

For all the background variables considered here, adjustment using the MCA model of the effects of the categories of a selected background variable leads to a significant reduction in these effects. The fine interplay of birth cohort and educational level may be noticed *(see Figure 4.4.)*. In the youngest cohort, the fertility of averagely and highly educated women is relatively low, while that of poorly educated women is relatively high. In the next cohort, poorly educated women have more children than averagely educated women, while the latter group has more children than highly educated women. The difference between highly and poorly educated women is pretty large: around 0.65 in both countries. In the birth cohort 1961-1965, Belgian women of each educational level on average have more children than Dutch women.

In the two older cohorts, an important difference between Belgium and the Netherlands is visible. The pattern of poorly educated women above averagely educated women and averagely educated women above highly educated women still applies in the Netherlands. The gap between poorly and highly educated women is about 0.4 children. In Belgium, however, the fertility of highly and poorly educated women is almost the same, while averagely educated women have fewer children (about 0.15). In the Netherlands, the lower fertility of highly educated women is usually related to the difficulties of combining motherhood with labour force participation. In Belgium, having children and having a paid job is very common. It might be possible that an income effect plays a role: highly educated women have more financial resources for raising children than averagely educated women, while poorly educated women more exclusively choose to be a mother.

The MCA model explains 40% of the total variance in the actual number of children in both countries. As was the case with expected childlessness, the explanatory power of MCA is drastically reduced by taking the expected number of children as a dependent variable: only 6% in Belgium and 11% in the Netherlands (see *Table 4.4.*). Again in this case, expected fertility has little to do with the selected background variables.

Women expect on average ultimately to have 2.0 children (see *Table 4.4.*). The pattern of the expectations (before correction) per birth cohort is not the same in Belgium and the Netherlands. Young cohorts of Belgian women expect slightly fewer children than older cohorts, while the relationship is reversed for their Dutch counterparts. In both countries, the expectations for single and cohabiting women are lower than for married women. The pattern of the effects of educational level again differs between the two countries. In Belgium, averagely educated women expect the fewest children and highly educated women expect the highest number, while the fertility of poorly educated women lies in between. In the Netherlands, both poorly and averagely educated women expect the same average family size, while that of highly educated women is much lower (0.23 children). The contrast between those who regularly to church regularly and those who are non-religious is large, especially in the Netherlands (0.64 children).

After correction by MCA, the effect of birth cohort on the expected number of children disappears in Belgium, while it has gained in importance in the Netherlands: young birth cohorts expect ultimately to have 0.4 more children than older cohorts. This seems very optimistic because the cumulated cohort fertility (at the ages that could be observed) has declined in the past (Vermunt, 1992).

Table 4.4. Expected number of children of women (MCA), Belgium, the Netherlands. Women born 1951-1970

	Belgium			the Netherlands			
	Unadjusted deviation **(Eta)**	Adjusted deviation **(Beta)**	Number of cases	Unadjusted deviation **(Eta)**	Adjusted deviation **(Beta)**	Number of cases	
Grand mean=1.98			3391			3686	Grand mean=2.03
Birth cohort		n.s.					Birth cohort
- 1966-1970	-0.11	0.01	746	0.07	0.22	951	- 1966-1970
- 1961-1965	-0.01	-0.02	944	0.05	0.05	969	- 1961-1965
- 1956-1960	0.07	0.03	913	-0.11	-0.11	913	- 1956-1960
- 1951-1955	0.03	-0.02	788	-0.18	-0.18	853	- 1951-1955
	(0.06)	(0.02)		(0.06)	(0.15)		
Living arrangement							Living arrangement
- single	-0.24	-0.26	752	-0.36	-0.41	904	- single
- cohabiting	-0.28	-0.16	303	-0.16	-0.15	561	- cohabiting
- married	0.11	0.11	2337	0.19	0.21	2221	- married
	(0.16)	(0.15)		(0.23)	(0.26)		
Educational level							Educational level
- low	0.00	-0.04	917	0.04	0.02	1399	- low
- medium	-0.11	-0.11	1246	0.04	0.02	1602	- medium
- high	0.11	0.14	1229	-0.19	-0.10	686	- high
	(0.09)	(0.10)		(0.09)	(0.04)		
Church attendance							Church attendance
- regular	0.21	0.20	782	0.49	0.46	330	- regular
- sometimes	0.12	0.09	1038	0.24	0.22	418	- sometimes
- seldom or never	-0.12	-0.11	940	0.02	0.00	1521	- seldom or never
- no religion	-0.28	-0.23	632	-0.21	-0.18	1417	- no religion
	(0.17)	(0.15)		(0.20)	(0.18)		
Explained variance=6%							Explained variance=11%

The effect of living arrangements is hardly changed by the correction: single women expect fewer children than cohabiting women, while married women expect more than cohabiting women. Also, the effects of church attendance are nearly the same after the correction: those of no religion expect fewer children.

Educational attainment has a slight influence on the expected number of children. In Belgium, highly educated women expect a larger family size than poorly and averagely educated women, while in the Netherlands, highly educated women expect a slightly smaller family size. Again, the conclusion is that the effect of education on fertility is largely a matter of timing, if we recall that the actual number of children differs substantially between educational levels. More highly educated women delay having children when they are younger although ultimately they want to have nearly the same size of family. So, in subsequent years, more highly educated women will try to catch up with the less well and averagely educated women.

4.6 Fertility of mothers

Both in Belgium and the Netherlands, mothers have an average of 2 children *(see Table 4.5.)*. In cohort 1966-1970, mothers have about 1.4 children, while mothers in cohort 1951-1955 have 2.1 children (Belgium) or 2.2 children (the Netherlands).

Unmarried cohabitation in the Netherlands has a significant negative effect on actual fertility. The actual family size of cohabiting Dutch women is 0.45 children smaller than that of married women; in Belgium it is 0.20 children smaller. The children of the single mothers were probably born when the mother was still married, after becoming single parents, these mothers probably would not have had any more children. Religious mothers have larger families than those who do not believe, especially in the Netherlands.
Labour force participation after the first birth has a slight effect in Belgium and a marked effect in the Netherlands. Dutch women who have (had) a paid job after the birth of the first child, have 0.29 fewer children than those who did not work after becoming a mother for the first time. In Belgium, this difference is only 0.14 children.

By considering the adjusted effects using the MCA model, a correct interpretation of the combined effects of birth cohort and educational level is possible. In the two youngest cohorts in both countries, poorly educated mothers have larger families than averagely or highly educated women *(see Figure 4.5)*. This is the same pattern as that of actual fertility for all women. In the two oldest cohorts in the Netherlands, there is hardly any difference between different educational levels. In Belgium, however, highly educated women have more children than poorly and averagely educated women. The pattern of the effects of the other background variables after adjustment using the MCA model is largely the same. The effect of labour participation is now the same in the two countries: those who have (had) a paid job after the birth of the first child have 0.2 fewer children than full-time mothers.

Figure 4.5. Actual number of children of mothers, by educational level and birth cohort, Belgium, the Netherlands. Mothers born 1951-1970

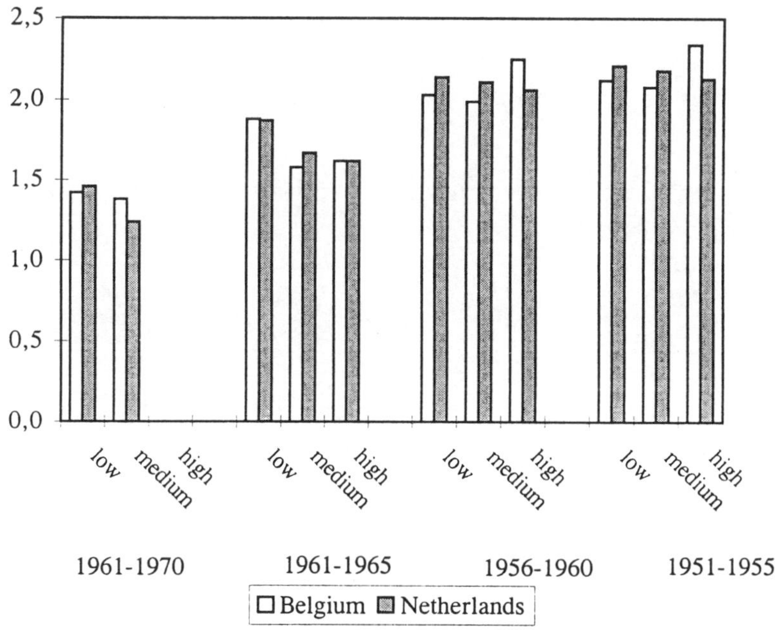

Table 4.5. Actual number of children of mothers (MCA), Belgium, the Netherlands. Mothers born 1951-1970

	Belgium			the Netherlands			
	Unadjusted deviation **(Eta)**	Adjusted deviation **(Beta)**	Number of cases	Unadjusted deviation **(Eta)**	Adjusted deviation **(Beta)**	Number of cases	
Grand mean = 1.92			2079			2008	Grand mean = 1.97
Birth cohort							Birth cohort
- 1966-1970	-0.57	-0.45	85	-0.63	-0.72	157	- 1966-1970
- 1961-1965	-0.28	-0.47	548	-0.25	-0.29	477	- 1961-1965
- 1956-1960	0.10	0.16	750	0.11	0.15	687	- 1956-1960
- 1951-1955	0.18	0.25	695	0.21	0.22	687	- 1951-1955
	(0.26)	(0.36)		(0.31)	(0.35)		
Living arrangement							Living arrangement
- single	-0.15	-0.13	137	-0.21	-0.23	181	- single
- cohabiting	-0.18	-0.05	108	-0.40	-0.21	108	- cohabiting
- married	0.02	0.01	1835	0.05	0.04	1720	- married
	(0.07)	(0.04)		(0.15)	(0.11)		
Educational level							Educational level
- low	0.05	-0.05	731	0.06	0.02	963	- low
- medium	-0.12	-0.09	760	-0.05	-0.01	767	- medium
- high	0.09	0.17	589	-0.07	-0.06	278	- high
	(0.11)	(0.12)		(0.07)	(0.03)		
Church attendance							Church attendance
- regular	0.19	0.16	483	0.47	0.44	200	- regular
- sometimes	0.04	0.03	705	0.26	0.41	250	- sometimes
- seldom or never	-0.13	-0.11	581	-0.07	-0.07	833	- seldom or never
- no religion	-0.14	-0.12	310	-0.14	-0.11	725	- no religion
	(0.15)	(0.13)		(0.24)	(0.21)		

Table 4.5. (continued) Actual number of children of mothers (MCA), Belgium, the Netherlands. Mothers born 1951-1970

	Belgium			the Netherlands			
	Unadjusted deviation **(Eta)**	Adjusted deviation **(Beta)**	Number of cases	Unadjusted deviation **(Eta)**	Adjusted deviation **(Beta)**	Number of cases	
Paid job after the first birth							Paid job after the first birth
- no	0.10	0.14	603	0.08	0.06	1438	- no
- yes	-0.04	-0.06	1477	-0.21	-0.15	570	- yes
	(0.08)	(0.10)		(0.16)	(0.11)		
Interactions: Birth cohort x Educational level							Interactions: Birth cohort x Educational level
- 1961-1965 x low	-0.04	0.48	162	-0.56	0.19	100	- 1966-1970 x low
	(0.01)	(0.16)		(0.16)	(0.05)		
- 1961-1965 x medium	-0.38	0.22	225	-0.13	0.17	204	- 1961-1965 x low
	(0.15)	(0.09)		(0.05)	(0.07)		
Explained variance = 11%							Explained variance = 18%

Only 11% (in Belgium) and 18% (in the Netherlands) of the total variance is explained by the regression model. If we are analysing the expected number of children of mothers, the regression model could scarcely determine important differences based on the selected background variables (see Table 4.6).

In all birth cohorts studied, mothers expect a final family size of 2.2 to 2.4 children. Single parents expect fewer children than married mothers. Religious mothers expect a larger family size than non-believers. Educational level and working situation after the first child do not have a significant effect on the expected number of children in the Netherlands. In Belgium highly educated women and women who do not work after the first child expect a higher number of children. Correction of the effects using the MCA model only leads to small changes.

4.7 Summary and discussion

The percentage of childless women, the average number of children per woman and the average number of children per mother do not differ much in Belgium and the Netherlands (*Figure 4.6*). This applies both to the realised and expected level of fertility. This would suggest that both countries are in the same stage of a common demographic transition process. A more detailed analysis, however, shows that there are significant differences between Belgium and the Netherlands.
The first stage of the Second Demographic Transition was characterised by a drastic decline in fertility. This stage has passed in both countries. The sharp decline in fertility was experienced by older generations than the cohorts that are analysed in the present study. This chapter focuses on the development in the fertility of young generations in the late stages of the transition process.

Figures on childlessness show that motherhood is postponed to higher ages in the Netherlands than in Belgium *(Figure 4.3)*. Especially Dutch highly educated women postpone having children. In the Netherlands over sixty percent of the highly educated women born in the period 1961-1965 were still childless at the time of the interview (they were around age thirty at the time) against fifty percent in Belgium, despite the fact that Dutch women were 1.5 years older at the time of the interview.

Table 4.6. Expected number of children of mothers (MCA), Belgium, the Netherlands. Mothers born 1951-1970

	Belgium			the Netherlands			
	Unadjusted deviation **(Eta)**	Adjusted deviation **(Beta)**	Number of cases	Unadjusted deviation **(Eta)**	Adjusted deviation **(Beta)**	Number of cases	
Grand mean = 2.23			2074			2008	Grand mean = 2.34
Birth cohort		n.s.					Birth cohort
- 1966-1970	0.03	0.08	85	0.07	0.09	157	- 1966-1970
- 1961-1965	-0.02	-0.02	548	0.10	0.10	477	- 1961-1965
- 1956-1960	0.02	0.00	750	0.01	0.00	687	- 1956-1960
- 1951-1955	0.00	0.00	691	-0.09	-0.09	687	- 1951-1955
	(0.02)	(0.02)		(0.09)	(0.09)		
Living arrangement							Living arrangement
- single	-0.21	-0.13	136	-0.29	-0.24	181	- single
- cohabiting	0.03	0.11	108	-0.11	-0.04	108	- cohabiting
- married	0.01	0.00	1832	0.04	0.03	1720	- married
	(0.06)	(0.05)		(0.12)	(0.10)		
Educational level					n.s.		Educational level
- low	-0.02	-0.05	729	-0.03	-0.01	963	- low
- medium	-0.11	-0.11	760	0.03	0.01	767	- medium
- high	0.18	0.20	587	0.00	0.03	278	- high
	(0.13)	(0.14)		(0.03)	(0.02)		
Church attendance							Church attendance
- regular	0.15	0.15	480	0.53	0.52	200	- regular
- sometimes	0.05	0.05	705	0.20	0.19	250	- sometimes
- seldom or never	-0.11	-0.11	581	-0.07	-0.07	833	- seldom or never
- no religion	-0.14	-0.15	309	-0.14	-0.13	725	- no religion
	(0.12)	(0.13)		(0.25)	(0.25)		

Table 4.6. (continued) Expected number of children of mothers (MCA), ***Belgium, the Netherlands.*** *Mothers born 1951-1970*

	Belgium			the Netherlands			
	Unadjusted deviation **(Eta)**	Adjusted deviation **(Beta)**	Number of cases	Unadjusted deviation **(Eta)**	Adjusted deviation **(Beta)**	Number of cases	
Paid job after the first birth					n.s.		Paid job after the first
- no	0.11	0.13	601	0.01	0.00	1438	birth
- yes	-0.04	-0.05	1474	-0.02	-0.01	570	- no
	(0.08)	(0.10)		(0.01)	(0.00)		- yes
Explained variance = 5%							Explained variance = 8%

Figure 4.6. Key fertility figures, Belgium, the Netherlands. Women born 1951-1970

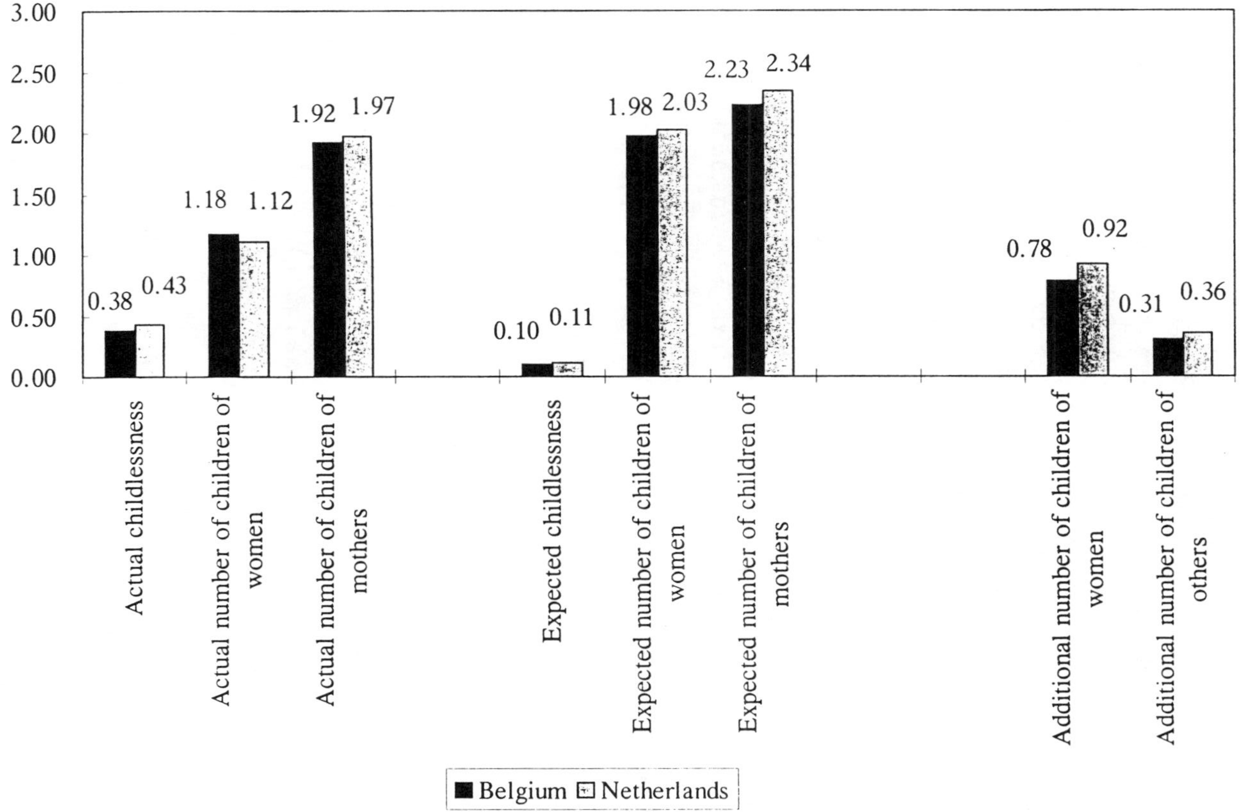

In both countries the level of educational attainment has a strong effect on having a first child: in the considered cohort the gap in the percentage of childlessness between women with poor and high levels of educational attainment amounts to 25 percentage points in Belgium and even to 30 percentage points in the Netherlands. For older cohorts the differences in childlessness by level of education are considerably smaller: 5 percentage points in Belgium and just over 10 percentage points in the Netherlands. Two possible interpretations spring to our mind. First, differences in childlessness by level of education may increase through time. This interpretation would imply that the final stage of the Second Demographic Transition has not yet been reached, as the differences between social groups are still widening. Second, the differences may be primarily due to the timing of fertility. This interpretation may be supported by the fact that considering expected childlessness rather than observed childlessness differences by educational level turn out to be very small. This applies to both countries, although more strongly to the Netherlands. This would mean that we are now in a stage of the Second Demographic Transition in which the timing rather than the ultimate level of fertility is changing. It should be emphasised however, that it is uncertain to what extent the expected level of fertility will become reality. For example, unwanted childlessness among highly educated women may increase due to infecundity as a result of postponement of births to higher ages.

The analysis of the actual number of children per woman also shows a strong effect of the level of educational attainment. Among women born in the period 1961-1965, in both countries the difference between women with low and high levels of education amounts to around 0.65 children *(Figure 4.4)*. Although the Dutch women were 1.5 year older at the time of the interview, in each educational category the number of children is lower than in Belgium. In the Netherlands among women of the oldest cohort the difference between lowly and highly educated amounts to 0.4 children. In Belgium, however, highly and poorly educated women have about the same number of children while women with a medium educational level have less children (about 0.15). The low fertility of highly educated women in the Netherlands may for the younger cohorts largely be a matter of timing. Differences in the expected ultimate number of children between the education categories are relatively small. Nevertheless in the Netherlands highly educated women expect a slightly lower family size. Moreover postponement of fertility may lead to a lower ultimate number of children than expected. Thus it is likely that the ultimate family size of highly educated women will be lower than that of poorly educated women.

By contrast, Belgian highly educated women expect to have slightly more children than women with an average or poor level of educational attainment. This may be explained by an income effect. Highly educated women have more financial resources to raise children than women with a lower level of educational attainment. In the Netherlands the relatively low fertility of highly educated women may be related to difficulties in combining motherhood with labour force participation.

References

Avramov, D., M. Callens and R. Cliquet (1995), Belgium: A Family-Friendly Climate as the Valorization of Individuality 81-101. In: H. Moors and R. Palomba (eds.), *Population, Family and Welfare. A comprehensive Survey of European Attitudes*. Oxford University Press.

Callens, M. and R. Schoenmaeckers (1993), Kinderen: hoeveel en wanneer? pp. 77-96. In: R.L. Cliquet and M. Callens (eds.), *Gezinsvorming in Vlaanderen: hoe en wanneer?*. Brussels: CBGS Monografie, 1.

Cruijsen, H. (1991), *Fertility in the European Community. Main trends, Recent Projections and Two Future Paths*. International Conference in Luxembourg 1991. Background papers on Fertility, Mortality and International Migration under Two Long Term Population Scenarios for the European Community. Luxembourg, Eurostat, pp. 1-30.

Graaf, A. de (1985) Onderzoek Gezinsvorming 1982: de keuze voor een kindertal. *Maandstatistiek van de Bevolking*, 33, 9, pp. 49-59.

Hoorn, W.D. van (1991), De invloed van werken van de vrouw op het aantal kinderen. *Maandstatistiek van de Bevolking*, 39, 10, pp. 17-26.

Jong, A.H. de (1987), Het eerste en tweede geboorte-interval nader belicht. *Maandstatistiek van de Bevolking*, 35, 5, pp. 14-23.

Jong, A.H. de (1998), *Long-Term Fertility scenarios for the countries of the European Economic Area*. EUROSTAT Working Papers, Population and social conditions, 3/1998/E/N° 17.

Kaa, D.J. van de (1993), The second demographic transition revisited: theories and expectations. 81-126. In: G. Beets et al. (eds.) *Population and Family in the Low Countries.*. Amsterdam/Lisse: Swets & Zeitlinger.

Lesthaeghe. R. and D.J. van de Kaa (1986), 'Twee demografische transities? In: D.J. van de Kaa and R. Lesthaeghe (eds.), *Bevolking: Groei en Krimp*. Deventer: Van Loghum Slaterus 9-24 (Mens en Maatschappij, Boekaflevering, vol. 61).

Lesthaeghe, R. and G. Verleye (1992), De tweede demografische transitie: Conceptuele basis en recente evolutie. In: *De demografische uitdaging: Nederland in Europa op weg naar de 21ste eeuw*, pp. 15-47.

Moors, H. (1995), The Netherlands: Great Tolerance but little Solidarity. 177-196. In: H. Moors and R. Palomba (eds.), *Population, Family and Welfare. A comprehensive Survey of European Attitudes*. Oxford University Press.

Moors, H. and R. Palomba (1995), Attitudes toward Marriage, Children and Population Policies in Europe.245-262. In: H. Moors and R. Palomba (eds.), *Population, Family and Welfare. A comprehensive Survey of European Attitudes*. Oxford University Press.

United Nations (1992), *Patterns of fertility in Low-Fertility Settings*. New York: Department of Economic and Social Development.

Vermunt, J.K. (1992), Geboorte: ontwikkelingen in het verleden en toekomstverwachtingen. *Maandstatistiek van de Bevolking*, 40, 1, 18-28.

5. LABOUR FORCE PARTICIPATION OF MOTHERS

Marc Callens, Wim van Hoorn, Andries de Jong

5.1 Introduction

Since the Second World War the labour force participation of women has increased across Western Europe. More recently, this development has been accompanied by the substitution of full-time jobs by part-time jobs. Characteristic of both trends is that women with children, who seldom used to go out to work, now are increasingly likely to have a paid job. In spite of this, the institutional diversity of the various member states of the European Union causes essential differences in the pattern of paid labour by women.

This chapter focuses on an analysis of the paid employment of Belgian and Dutch women aged 20-39. For various family formation stages, i.e. before the first child and after each of the first three births, separate MCA analyses are performed to find out to what extent labour force participation and part-time employment are influenced by factors such as the period of children's births, age of the mother when children are born, and the educational level and church attendance of the woman.

5.2 Context

5.2.1 Labour force participation in a historical perspective

After the Second World War the reconstruction process and the subsequent increased prosperity in Western Europe led to a growing demand for labour. It did not result in a sharp increase in the labour force participation of

J. de Beer and F. Deven (eds.), Diversity in Family Formation, 89–113.

women since the lack of manpower was compensated by recruiting foreign workers from the Mediterranean countries.

In the Netherlands in particular, it remained unusual for married women - and certainly for mothers - to work (just after the war, female civil servants were even obliged to resign when they married). This low labour force participation until the mid-sixties was bound up with a role pattern which was still rather traditional. While, in other European countries, secularisation was in full swing, 'compartmentalisation' froze social processes in the Netherlands. Furthermore, legislation also discouraged women from working.

Figure 5.1 illustrates the evolution of the activity profile for women in Belgium and the Netherlands from 1961-1991. As in other countries in the European Union, the activity rate of 25-49 year-old women has risen strongly in recent decades (Commission of the European Communities, 1993). This development largely reflects the increased labour force participation of women with children.

At the beginning of the nineteen-sixties, the female activity profiles of both countries show the same basic form: a curve with one (high) peak for 20-25 year-olds, about equal for the two countries, and increasingly lower activity rates for the older age groups. This corresponds to a situation in which women stop working as soon as they marry and/or when they have children. But that is where the similarity between Belgium and the Netherlands ends, as the activity rate of older age groups is extremely low in the latter country. With a rate of 16% for 30-34 year-old women, the Netherlands finds itself in the company of Spain and Portugal in the European Union, while Belgium, with 33% for this age group, is in the middle group. The highest activity rates for this age group (40% and over) are observed in Denmark, France, the United Kingdom and Germany (Commission of the European Communities, 1993).

Figure 5.1. Activity rates for women, by age group. Belgium and the Netherlands, 1961-1991

Belgium

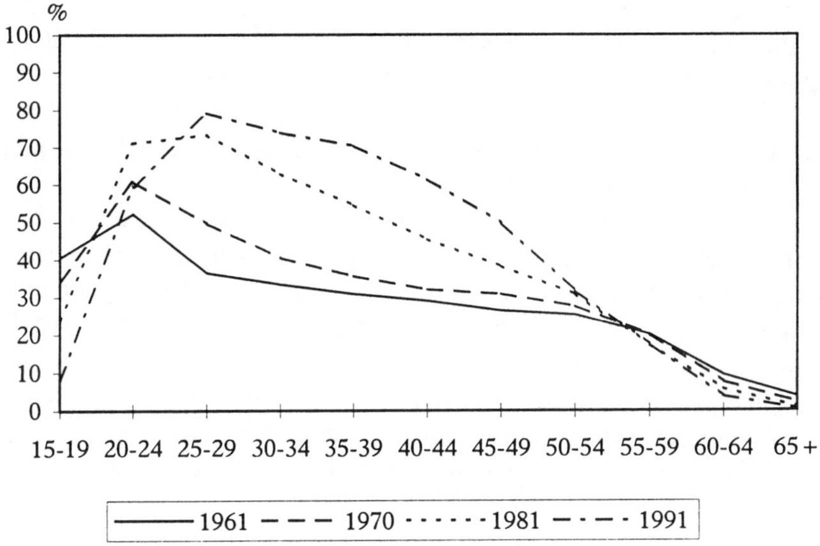

the Netherlands

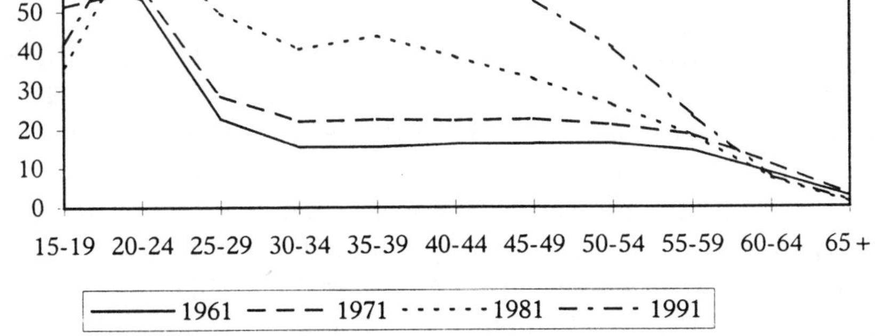

Sources: Commission of the European Communities, ILO (Yearbook of labour statistics); Eurostat, Community Labour Force Survey.

The activity profile of Dutch women in 1981 has a double peak, indicating a pattern of (temporary) interruption of the working career, followed by re-entry into the labour force. In 1991, the second peak has disappeared. In Belgium, on the other hand, the female activity curve is gradually approaching the male bell form, which indicates a career without interruption (Ministry of Labour and Employment, 1994). The activity rate for 30-34 year-old Dutch women has risen fourfold since 1960 to 61% which brings it level with Belgium in the middle European group in this respect.

Various factors underlie this rise in labour force participation. Far-reaching industrialisation has increased the demand for labour. The growth of the services and caring sectors, where women are relatively strongly represented, has encouraged many women to start or keep working. Furthermore, it is now less the norm for women to care for the home and family on a full-time basis and not to have a paid job. Social processes such as secularisation, emancipation and individualisation are increasing. Higher wages are making it more worthwhile for women —especially more highly educated women— to go out to work, leaving others to care for their children. The increase in the number of part-time jobs and —at a later stage— the extension of child-care facilities have contributed to this.

The two countries display essential differences when the activity rates of women are related to the number of children (*Figure 5.2*). As for other EU countries, the activity rate decreases at every age with the number of children. In Belgium, the difference in activity rate remains relatively small between women with no children or one or two children; it is remarkably lower for women with three children. In the Netherlands, the break is between women with no children and those with one child.

5.2.2 Part-time labour

Female labour force participation has risen rapidly in Northern Europe since the late 1950s. To a large extent, it refers to part-time labour. Depending on the context, two stages can be distinguished: the first lasting until the early nineteen-seventies, the second starting at the time of the first oil crisis and still continuing now. In both periods the integration of married women into the labour market is the essential process. Before the first oil crisis, this integration process occurred within a context of a declining supply of young unmarried women, combined with a growing demand for female labour (Blossfeld and Rohwer 1993). After the oil crisis, this integration continued - in spite of the high unemployment rates.

Figure 5.2.Activity rates for women, by age group and actual number of children. Belgium and the Netherlands, 1988

Belgium

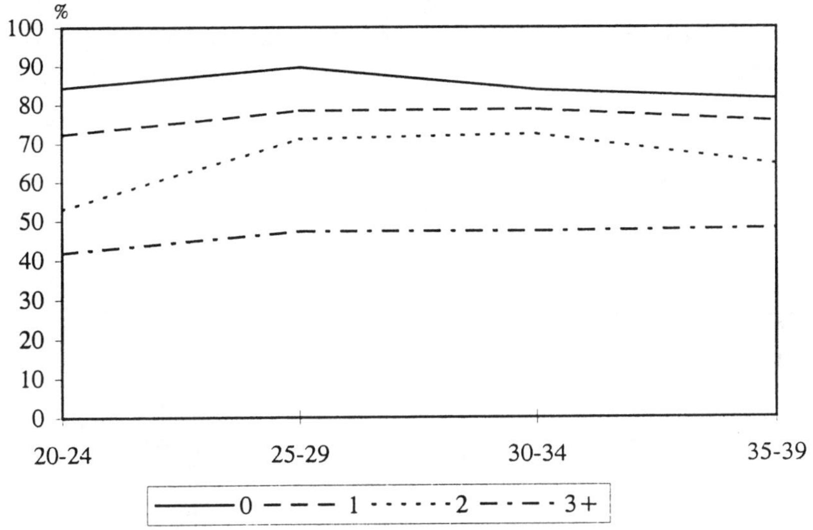

the Netherlands

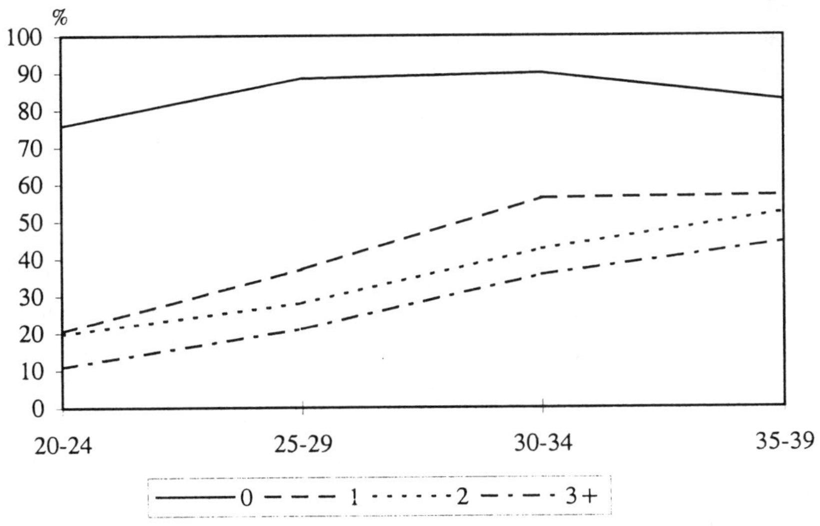

With an overall percentage of 25% part-time employment of working women in 1987, Belgium was a middle-group country in the European Union. The Netherlands, on the other hand, had the highest level (60%). Broken down by family status, it turns out that in 1991 nine out of ten Dutch working women with children work part-time (*see Figure 5.3*). This is significantly more than single women without children (37%). In Belgium too, working women with children more often have a small job than single women without children (35% versus 15%).

Figure 5.3. Women in part-time employment, by family status. Belgium and the Netherlands, 1991

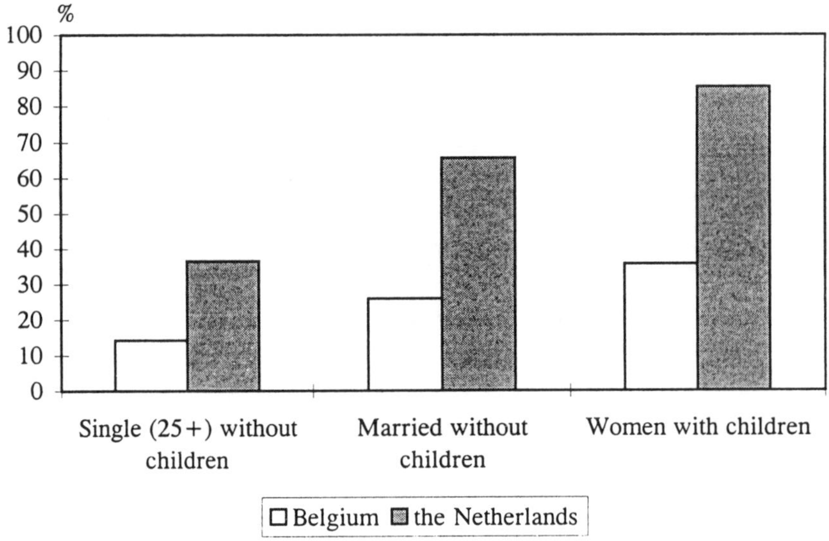

Source: Community Labour Force Survey.

The two stages mentioned above can indeed be discerned in the development of part-time labour in Belgium. Up to the end of the nineteen-sixties, many people started to work part-time voluntarily. The employment crisis of the nineteen-seventies changed the structure of part-time employment radically as it became a matter of redistribution of labour and of flexibility. This form of —involuntary— part-time employment is especially characterised by the presence of weak groups on the labour market (women, young people, the poorly educated) (Ramioul, 1993).

The Belgian government has actively promoted part-time employment; since 1981 it has been integrated into labour legislation and social security provisions. These measures especially encourage the voluntary form of part-time employment. Other labour redistributive measures were taken, the most important being the system of 'part-time labour to combat unemployment'. This measure grants a supplementary unemployment benefit to anyone who is unemployed and who accepts a part-time job. On becoming unemployed again, he or she will receive full unemployment benefit. The number of beneficiaries under this scheme rose phenomenally from 20,000 in 1982 to 200,000 in 1989 (Holderbeke, 1991). Under pressure from diminishing public funds, the federal government reformed the system considerably in 1993, making it less attractive. It is expected that this will slow down the growth in part-time employment (Callens, 1995).

In the Netherlands, the increasing tendency of married women to get a job, the demand for labour, especially in the services sector and - more recently - the demand for the flexibilisation of labour have all reinforced each other to lead to a rapid increase in the number of women working part-time.

Dutch government policy on part-time labour has always been strongly dominated by emancipation policy (SCP, 1993), although increasing numbers of women were working part-time before any official policy existed. In 1976 an interdepartmental working group "Emancipation and part-time labour as aspects of government policy", was set up which recommended, among other things, making part-time employment possible in higher positions. In the early nineteen-eighties, certain subsidies were granted to promote part-time employment in the private sector. This experiment was not continued, however, because the subsidised jobs were not created in new economic sectors. As in Belgium, in the Netherlands provision is made for people who have become unemployed and can only find a job with reduced hours. If the job is for fewer hours than the most recent job, they retain part of their unemployment benefit.

The government "has taken it upon itself to support to a certain extent the growth, distribution and quality of part-time employment, but thinks that the promotion of part-time labour is mainly the task of market processes and market parties" (Tweede Kamer der Staten Generaal, 1994). According to the government, social security legislation forms no obstacle to part-time work. However, "a legal provision will be made (to be included in the Civil Code) which forbids discrimination against employees on the grounds of differences in hours worked and grants exemption only if and in so far as the discrimination is objectively justifiable". The 1/3 criterion in the Minimum Wage Act (and Minimum Holiday Allowance Act) has been cancelled, so that people who work for less than the equivalent of 1/3 of a job are also entitled to a minimum wage.

5.2.3 The welfare state: childcare

A strong determinant for the labour market participation of women in any country is the way in which differences between men and women are institutionalised in the welfare state, i.e. in the wage structure, systems of social security and in the way care for the elderly, the ill and children is organised (Plantenga and van Doorne-Huiskens, 1993).

Several typologies have been developed to describe this. One distinguishes two types of social arrangement: the Swedish arrangement and the traditional arrangement. The former comprises good facilities in the field of childcare and parental leave and a situation where the state has taken over much of the caring responsibility. The traditional arrangement is based on the distinction between the breadwinner and the housewife (Huisman and Pot, 1987). The typology developed by Esping-Andersen (1991) distinguishes three types of welfare state: (1) social democratic, (2) liberal and (3) conservative. It is mainly based on the extent to which the welfare state guarantees individual subsistence, independent of market processes.

The typology developed by Plantenga and van Doorne-Huiskens (1993) retains the basic classification of Esping-Andersen and, additionally, explains the extent to which a subsistence exists alongside or outside the family. In pursuit of the highest possible level of equality between civilians and of total employment for men and women, in the social democratic welfare state an important share of the caring activities are taken over by the public sector (e.g. Denmark). An extensive childcare network maximises labour market participation. In the conservative/corporative welfare state (e.g. Germany) the family is seen as an anchor for societal stability: men are breadwinners, women stay at home and look after the family. In this philosophy, childcare is unnecessary; the role of the state is restricted to (financial) compensation via facilities for breadwinners. In the liberal welfare state (e.g. Great Britain) the level of social provision is low and there are hardly any childcare facilities.

The Netherlands combines social democratic elements (high level of income redistribution) with conservative/corporative elements (facilities for working mothers - especially childcare - are underdeveloped). Belgium too can be considered as a combination of social democratic and conservative/corporative elements: in spite of high industrial development and a strong welfare state (including an extensive system of childcare), Belgium has only an average position as far as the economic position of women is concerned. This is mainly because both the social partners and the government have always started out from a traditional model with the man as breadwinner (Triest, 1993).

As far as childcare facilities are concerned, Belgium and the Netherlands occupy extreme positions in Europe. Only Denmark scores higher than Belgium for the percentage of places for under-threes. The Netherlands, on the other hand, has a low score (Goedhart et al., 1992).

Since 1987, Dutch childcare policy has changed drastically. A stimulation policy has been pursued and funds have been reserved to extend the care facilities for toddlers and infants, with the underlying motive of increasing the possibilities for parents to combine having children with a paid job. Indeed, since 1988, the number of professional childcare places has risen from fewer than 20,000 to some 60,000 (European Commission Network on Childcare, 1996).

One important element in the structure of childcare in the Netherlands is the participation of the social partners (Ministerie van WVC, 1992). An increasing proportion of childcare places are rented to employers. If a company hires a place, it is entitled to a municipal reduction. Hiring places at an existing centre is more common than setting up an in-house company crèche. About 20% of existing childcare facilities are not subsidised. The government reduced the subsidies in January 1996. The premium system was abolished and replaced by a tax exemption for companies for 25% of the costs they incur for childcare. This can be seen as a change of course towards liberalism.

OG'93 reveals that only one quarter of working mothers with children under 4 years of age use professional childcare (day-care centre or an official childminder). Most women still take their children to a relative or have a paid baby-sitter at home. Some mothers who do not have a paid job also use professional facilities (around 10% of the total capacity).
In Belgium, half of children aged under 3 are cared for by grandparents or other relatives, one quarter attend day-care centres and one quarter go to childminders. In addition to day-care centres and playgroups, there is an extensive system of private childminders in Belgium. Care facilities within

companies or subsidised by companies are still very limited (e.g. Buysse et al., 1997, Deven, 1998).

5.3 Theory

5.3.1 Economic theories and the role of education

In neo classic economic theory, children are seen as durable goods. Since money is needed to raise children, there is a positive relationship between working and having children. In Becker's (1981) New Home Economics, children cost both time and money. Since men's wages are usually higher than those of their wives, while their productivity in the home is usually lower, there will be a strong tendency for the woman to concentrate on housework while the man has a paid job. This means that the presence of children has a negative effect on the labour supply of women (e.g. Siegers, 1985). As the children grow up, the cost in time decreases while financial costs increase (Wiebrens, 1981), weakening the negative relationship and turning the effect into a positive one (Henkens et al., 1993).
The peculiar development of labour participation in the Netherlands - very low for a long time followed by a sharp rise - cannot be explained by this theory. Belgium fits in more closely with the more "normal" development, at least in a European perspective.
Indeed, alternative theories have been developed for the Netherlands, taking into account the country's inheritance from the past - relative prosperity meant that it was possible for Dutch women to stay at home and devote themselves to bringing up the children (Pott-Buter 1993, 1994) - and the dominance of the so-called social 'household norm' until the early sixties: mothers were not supposed to work (Vendrik; 1993, 1994).

In the 'human capital' theory (Gustafsson, 1991), education is seen as an investment for the labour market career. The higher the educational level, the more attractive participation in the labour market will be. According to Sperber et al. (1980), highly educated women looking for a job take other matters into account than purely financial motives: they want to make use of their own talents, to lead an interesting life as well as having independence. For these reasons, they are more career-oriented than their less well educated peers (Mott and Shapiro, 1983). Consequently, the opportunity costs of children will rise as women are more likely to have work which is financially attractive and professionally satisfying. The higher their education, the more attractive labour market participation is and the less satisfying looking after the household and children will be.

The variable 'education' is also often linked with a complex of background characteristics. According to Vermunt (1991), education is the most important indicator of an underlying dimension called 'lifestyle'. Education gives people a wider perspective (De Jong-Gierveld and Beekink, 1989). This means people are open to new ideas and behaviour patterns. Emancipation, secularisation and individualisation processes were in fact quick to occur among the more highly educated. De Feijter (1990) links education with innovative value patterns. In the Netherlands, these are mainly observed among a small group of highly educated, economically well-off non-religious young people. These 'innovators' value paid employment very highly. After a time, their behaviour and lifestyles are copied by other groups. This means that differences in work behaviour between more highly and less well educated people increasingly reduce and that the less well educated make up for their relative disadvantage in labour market participation (Bernhardt, 1986).
The motivation of less well educated women for labour market participation has a different character and is mainly a consequence of financial and material needs (De Vries, 1993). If these could be fulfilled in another way, the motivation to be economically active would probably be low. Lack of qualifications for the labour market and sensitivity to social pressure towards adopting a traditional lifestyle add to this. Groot and Jehoel-Gijsbers, (1989) mention another effect of education on the rate of labour participation: the more highly educated also have more opportunities on the labour market.

5.3.2 Explanatory variables

It is apparent from the above that education can be seen as a sort of summary indicator of background characteristics such as lifestyle, income, social position and level of ambition. This variable will therefore be an important factor in the analysis of labour participation on the basis of data from OG'93 and NEGO V. We shall look into whether it does indeed have such a strong effect on having a job as the literature suggests (Pauwels et al., 1988; Mertens et al., 1992).

Religiousness, measured in terms of church attendance, is a socio-cultural explanatory value. Willingness to conform to prevalent values and norms is related to religiousness (e.g. Lesthaege and Meekers, 1987). It is then to be expected that non-religious women with children will more often have a job than religious mothers. Considering the different religious situations in the Netherlands and Belgium, it will be interesting to see whether the effect of this variable is the same for both countries.

The mother's age at the birth of her children is one of the two demographic explanatory variables in the analyses. Increased age when the first child is born is often seen as 'modern' behaviour and it would therefore seem logical to link it with a relatively high labour participation rate (e.g. De Jong, 1995; CBS, 1994). There is also an economic reason for older mothers to keep their jobs: they have already invested too much in their career to give it up.

In view of the fact that, especially in the Netherlands, so much has changed with respect to working mothers over the past few years, the variable 'period of birth' has also been included in the analyses.

Both surveys contain the Inglehart scale which measures (post-)material attitudes. Due to the lack of significant effects, it is not used in the definite models.

5.4 Data collection and analysis techniques

The issue of 'working women' is not approached identically by the two surveys. The OG‘93 concentrates on the relationship with the birth of a child. The NEGO V asks for the complete working history; based on this the work situation around the birth of children can be reconstructed. Having a job 9 months before and 12 months after the birth of a child are used to produce results comparable to those of the OG.

OG'93 defines hours of work as follows. A full-time job is a job of at least 32 hours; a part-time job is one of 12 to 31 hours. If women have jobs for fewer hours, which hardly occurs, they are counted as not working. In NEGO V a part-time job is a job for half the normal number of hours worked; a full-time job includes all jobs with hours between half the number of hours and the normal number of hours worked. As OG'93 was carried out later than NEGO V, the variable 'period of birth' has one more category in the Netherlands than in Belgium.
The analysis technique used is the multiple classification analysis (MCA). This is a multivariate regression technique specifically appropriate in the case of nominal explanatory variables. Per category of each explanatory factor, both an unadjusted and an adjusted percentage of working mothers are calculated. The corrected values reflect the 'inherent' influence of every explanatory variable on working. The term *'eta'* in the tables shows for every explanatory factor what the (bivariate) correlation is with the dependent variable; the beta is the partial correlation coefficient. The total explained vari-

ance shows which part of the differences in the dependent variable are explained by all explanatory factors together (see *Technical Appendix*).
The analyses looked for any significant interaction effects of the explanatory variables on the labour force participation of women. For the Netherlands, this was the case only once and it will be dealt with within context. Elsewhere, we shall not mention the lack of significant interaction effects.

5.5 Results

5.5.1 Working before the first child is born

Labour force participation. Before the birth of the first child there are few differences between Dutch and Belgian women as far as labour force participation is concerned. During this life cycle stage, nearly all women go out to work for a certain period. In Belgium and the Netherlands, 98% of women have had a job at some time. This means that the level of education has hardly any differentiating effect at the start of the career.

A minority of women stop working before they have children, for example, when they get married or start cohabiting. Both in Belgium and the Netherlands, some 20% of women have given up their job before becoming pregnant for the first time. More highly educated women are less likely to give up their jobs than those with a poorer education. Religiousness is apparently of little significance in this respect.
In Belgium, the impact of the economic cycle is visible and reflected as a U-shaped curve. In the period 1982-1984 having a low economic growth rate 73% of women had a job. During the 'booming' 1960s and 1970s, this was just over 80%. In 1988-1990 the economic growth rate was high again and the proportion of active women rose to 87%. No other significant differentiations were observed.

Part-time labour. In Belgium and the Netherlands alike, women who become pregnant for the first time more often have a full-time job. In the Netherlands, one third of pregnant women work part-time. In 1990, one fifth of Flemish women with a job worked part-time when they became pregnant for the first time. Ten to twenty years ago, this was just one in thirty women.

5.5.2 Working after the birth of the first child

Labour force participation. The Netherlands has seen a sharp rise in the labour force participation of women after the birth of their first child in recent decades. While at the end of the nineteen-seventies, only one woman in ten went back to work after the birth of her first child, by the early nineteen-nineties, nearly half of first-time mothers went back to work. (see *Table 5.1*). The mother's age when her first child is born has a clear effect on the proportion of working women. Combining work with a child is not popular among young mothers - fewer than one in five go back to work, while half of mothers aged thirty or over go back. As expected, educational level also has a significant effect on paid employment. Only one in five less well educated women go back to work, again compared with half of more highly educated women. Lastly, religiousness also plays a part: non-religious women work slightly more often than those who attend church services regularly.

In Belgium, labour force participation of mothers after the birth of their first child has been a matter of course for a much longer time. In the 1960s and 1970s, two out of three of first-time mothers went back to work; by the late 1980s, three-quarters did so. As far as the effect of age when the first child is born is concerned, Belgium is very similar to the Netherlands. The activity rate of young mothers drops to 60%, while 80% of those who have their baby later go back to work. In the Netherlands and in Belgium alike, four fifths of more highly educated mothers work after the birth of their first child. For mothers with a lower education this is the case for just over half.

In the multivariate MCA the 'corrected' figures clearly reveal fewer differences than the 'uncorrected' ones. This is due to the relationships between the explanatory variables. Among more highly educated women, for example, the age when their first child is born is usually high because the birth of the child is postponed so that the woman can complete her studies and then put her skills into practise in a (full-time) job for a few years. Moreover, over the past decades, increasing numbers have been enrolling in higher education. There is therefore a certain relationship with the period of birth of the first child.

The effect of the mother's age when children are born becomes noticeably smaller, especially in the Dutch multivariate model. The difference between the highest and lowest category drops from 40 to 23 percentage points. For period of birth and education, clear reductions in differences between the categories are also clear (from 39 to 24 percentage points and 33 to 21 percentage points respectively). For church attendance, the corrected and uncorrected figures differ much less. In the Belgian multivariate model the differences are analogous, although less pronounced; the period effect is completely eliminated.

Table 5.1. Mothers who have a paid job after the birth of their first child (%)[1]

MCA analysis	The Netherlands			Belgium		
	unadjusted	adjusted	number of cases	unadjusted	adjusted	number of cases
grand mean:	27		1971	69		1875
Period of first birth						
- before 1978	10	19	392	66	74	524
- 1979-1981	15	19	284	67	68	304
- 1982-1984	23	24	318	66	64	351
- 1985-1987	28	25	339	72	68	327
- 1988-1990	41	35	376	75	68	339
- 1991-1993	49	43	262	-	-[3]	-
	eta=.31	beta=.19		eta=.08	beta=.07	ns[2]
Age at first birth						
- < 25	13	19	865	62	63	1124
- 25-29	33	31	815	81	79	649
- >= 30	53	42	290	75	72	71
	eta=.31	beta=.18		eta=.20	beta=.16	
Educational level						
- low	18	22	948	55	57	608
- medium	30	28	755	72	73	692
- high	51	43	267	81	78	545
	eta=.25	beta=.15		eta=.22	beta=.19	
Church attendance						
- regular						
- sometimes	17	19	318	69	69	445
- seldom or never	29	27	371	70	70	629
- no religion	27	28	549	68	68	504
	31	30	732	68	68	266
	eta=.10	beta=.08		eta=.02	beta=.03	ns
Explained variance:		16%			7%	

[1] Working time at least 12 hours (the Netherlands) and at least half-time (Belgium)
[2] ns: not significant; $p>0.05$
[3] Data are not available for Belgium.

In the Dutch model, there seems to be a significant interaction effect of education and age when children are born on working. Although highly educated women who give birth after their thirtieth birthday often return to work, this is still less than according to the combined main effects of both factors. In other words, the combination of high education/late motherhood has a smaller effect than if both effects were added together.

Part-time labour. In Belgium, 82% of the 20-39 year-old first-time mothers work full-time. Compared to the period 1960-1978, part-time jobs are now five times as popular (6% versus 32%). Older, highly educated liberal and post-materialistic women work part-time more often than the average.

The Dutch part-time/full-time ratio mirrors the Belgian case: mothers with one child more often work part-time (77%). The increase in part-time labour has been significant. About half of mothers of children born before 1978 worked part-time. For mothers giving birth in the period 1985-1990, this had already risen to 80% (*see Figure 5.4*). For 1991-1993, the percentage is slightly lower. This again illustrates the increasing popularity of part-time labour in the Netherlands; as in Belgium, it is less frequent among women who have children later and among highly educated women.

Figure 5.4. Percentage of mothers who work part-time, by period of birth. Belgium and the Netherlands*

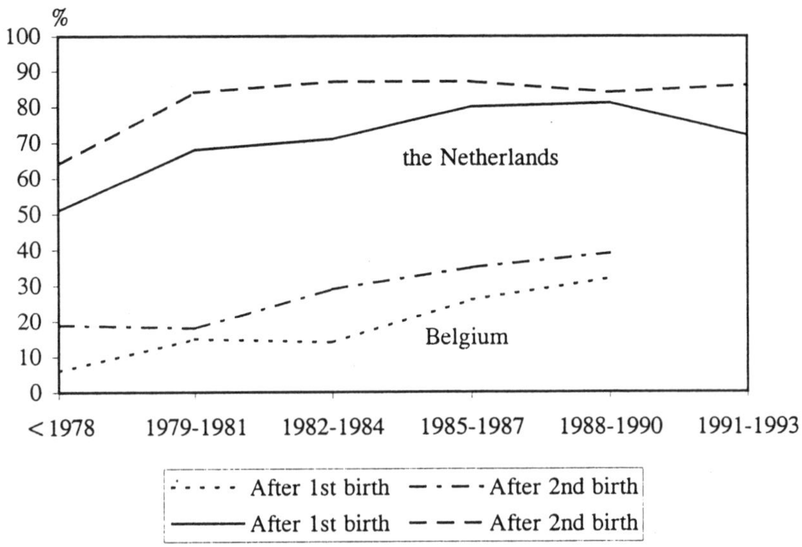

* less than 32 hours. Belgium not available in 1991-1993

Multivariate analysis of the number of part-timers among working women reveals that, both in the Netherlands and Belgium, only the period of birth has an apparent effect. This seems to signify that for young Dutch mothers, the primary decision is whether or not to keep their job. Once they have made that choice, the number of hours they work depends mainly on personal circumstances. For Belgium, it seems to be less clear-cut. Liberalism and a high level of education show a weak non-significant relationship with a preference for part-time work. In view of the small number of observations included in the analysis, the possibility of a certain structure in the data cannot be ruled out.

5.5.3 Working after the birth of the second child

Labour force participation. Labour force participation after the birth of the second child is illustrated in *Table 5.2.* For the Netherlands, as in the case of the first child, there is a clear period effect. Before 1980, only one woman in ten had a job after the birth of her second child, compared to one third of women in the period 1988-1993. The age of the mother when the second child is born also has a clear effect. Among mothers younger than 25, one in ten work following the birth of their second child, compared to one in three among those over 30. As expected, the level of education retains a strong influence on paid work, while religiousness also plays a part. Twelve percent of less well educated women work after their second child is born, compared to 45% of more highly educated women. Non-religious mothers work slightly more often than those who regularly attend church services.

In Belgium too, the bivariate distribution seems to show a period effect. Up to 24% more women who have had their second child recently go back to work, compared to the situation before 1978. Having a second child and having it when young are combined by one woman in three. Twice as many mothers have their second child when they are older. The strongest effect is that of educational level. Nearly four out of five highly educated women remain economically active after the birth of their second child. For less well educated women, this is less than two out of five.

In the Dutch MCA analyses, the effects of the explanatory variables are reduced in the same way as for the first child, i.e. the scores are nearer the general average. In the Belgian multivariate model, only the effect of education remains.

Part-time labour. Nearly 30% of the working mothers in the NEGO survey opt for a part-time job after the birth of their second child (at the end of the 1980s the figure was 40%, whereas in 1960-1978 it was only 20%). This figure is much higher than that after the birth of the first child (18%).

Table 5.2. Mothers who have a paid job after the birth of their second child (%)[1]

MCA-analysis	the Netherlands			Belgium		
	unadjusted	adjusted	number of cases	unadjusted	adjusted	numbe[illegible] of case[illegible]
grand mean:	21		1400	58		116[illegible]
Period of second birth						
- before 1978	10	16	162	42	57	16[illegible]
- 1979-1981	8	13	184	54	57	23[illegible]
- 1982-1984	18	20	234	60	60	23[illegible]
- 1985-1987	18	18	308	62	58	27[illegible]
- 1988-1990	30	26	281	66	58	26[illegible]
- 1991-1993	36	31	231	-	-[3]	
	eta=.24	beta=.15		eta=.16	beta=.02	ns
Age at second birth						
- < 25	10	15	310	38	46	34[illegible]
- 25-29	17	19	667	65	62	66[illegible]
- >= 30	36	29	423	72	67	15[illegible]
	eta=.25	beta=.13		eta=.26	beta=.17	
Educational level						
- low	12	14	712	36	39	39[illegible]
- medium	25	24	509	61	61	39[illegible]
- high	45	40	179	78	75	37[illegible]
	eta=.27	beta=.21		eta=.35	beta=.30	
Church attendance						
- regular	13	15	259	56	57	31[illegible]
- sometimes	25	22	286	57	56	42[illegible]
- seldom or never	21	23	371	57	57	27[illegible]
- no religion	23	22	485	67	66	15[illegible]
	eta=.10	beta=.08		eta=.07	beta=.07	n[illegible]
Explained variance:		13%			15%	

[1] Working time at least 12 hours (the Netherlands) and at least half-time (Belgium)
[2] ns: not significant; p>0.05
[3] Data are not available for Belgium.

Some 85% of Dutch mothers with two children who work have a part-time job. This is more than 10 percentage points higher than after the birth of the first child. Here too, compared to the period before 1978, the share of part-timers grew most sharply (see *Figure 5.4*). Both in the Netherlands and in Belgium, the background characteristics do not have a significant effect on the full-time/part-time ratio.

5.5.4 Working after the birth of a third child

Labour force participation. After the birth of their third child, 17% of Dutch mothers have a paid job. The MCA analysis of labour participation after the birth of the third child gives roughly the same results as for the second child (*Table 5.3*). The effects of the period and age when the child is born are about the same as for the second child, but the effect of education is even stronger. Only 7% of mothers with three children and a low educational level work compared to 41% of those with a high educational level. Religiousness also affects the labour force participation of mothers with three children: the activity rate for non-religious mothers is 10 percentage points higher than that for regular churchgoers.

In Belgium, about 45 percent of mothers remain active after the birth of their third child. This is still more than after the birth of a first child in the Netherlands. Education has a strong effect here (*beta*=.43). In Belgium, up to three-quarters of highly educated women go back to work after their third child; this is barely fewer than after the second or first child. Less well educated women go back to work much less often (<25%) after their third baby. Other effects, such as that of period of birth and mother's age, are completely neutralised in the multivariate model by the effect of education. In view of the small number of observations, caution should, however, be exercised.

Part-time labour. In Belgium, part-time jobs are just as popular as full-time ones among mothers with three children. Highly educated mothers can to some extent attribute their higher activity rates to the - mainly recent - strategy of more often working part-time. In the Netherlands, nearly 90% of working mothers who had their third child around 1990 have a part-time job (that is an additional 5 percentage points more than after the second child). For working mothers who had their third child before 1978, this percentage was much lower. The data cannot be interpreted further due to the low number of observations.

5.5.5 Main factors: education and parity

Before drawing any conclusions, it seems relevant to combine the main results of the separate analyses, specifically the strong characteristic factor of parity and the dominant role of educational level.

Table 5.3. Mothers who have a paid job after the birth of their third child(%)[1]

MCA-analysis	the Netherlands			Belgium		
	unajusted	adjusted	number of cases	unadjusted	adjusted	number of cases
grand mean:	17		429	45		313
Period of third birth						
- before 1978	[4]			7	29	18
- 1979-1981	8	15	43	41	46	45
- 1982-1984	5	6	68	47	46	70
- 1985-1987	13	14	95	54	49	91
- 1988-1990	19	16	120	43	43	89
- 1991-1993	30	26	80		[3]	
	eta=.22	beta=.16		eta=.16	beta=.09	ns
Age at second birth						
- < 25	1	6	32	18	37	44
- 25-29	10	13	194	47	46	180
- >= 30	24	20	203	54	48	88
	eta=.22	beta=.12	ns	eta=.23	beta=.07	ns[2]
Educational level						
- low	7	9	209	22	23	116
- medium	21	20	167	39	39	91
- high	41	38	53	76	74	106
	eta=.31	beta=.26		eta=.46	beta=.43	
Church attendance						
- regular	11	12	133	49	49	104
- sometimes	20	17	83	44	43	111
- seldom or never	16	17	95	42	43	70
- no religion	22	21	118	38	42	27
	eta=.13	beta=.10	ns	eta=.07	beta=.06	ns
Explained variance:		16%			24%	

[1] Working time at least 12 hours (the Netherlands) and at least half-time (Belgium)

[2] ns: not significant; $p>0.05$

[3] Data are not available for Belgium

[4] N<15

Set side by side, the separate analyses show clearly how important the number of young children is for the labour participation of mothers. In Belgium, there is a gradual decrease in labour participation from 80% (just after completing education) to just under 50% following the birth of the third child (*Figure 5.5*). In the Netherlands, the sharpest drop (from 80% to below 30%) occurs when the first child is born.

For Dutch women, the effect of the mother's age on working decreases to some extent for the higher parity levels. It may be that it is more difficult to combine children and a paid job, in spite of childcare facilities.

Figure 5.5. Working women at different stages in the life cycle (%) Belgium and the Netherlands

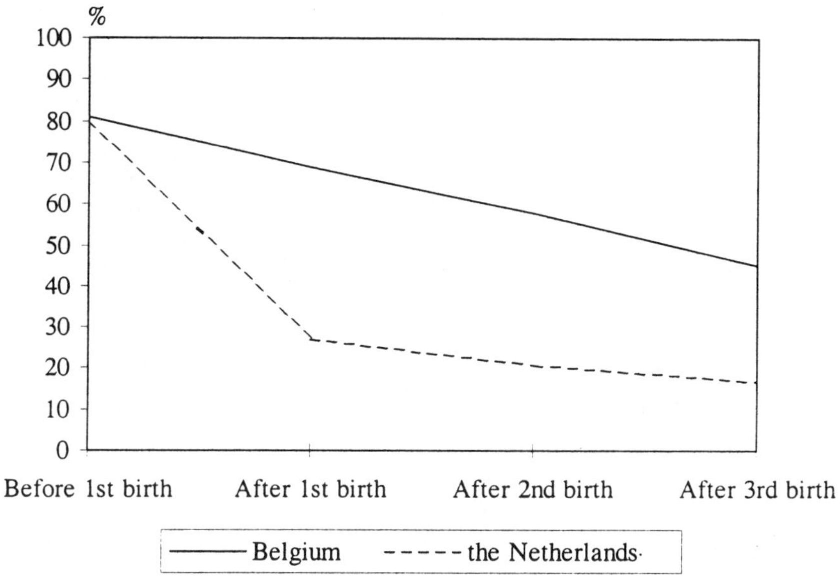

Figure 5.6. Effect of education on labour force participation of women; betas in MCA-analysis, Belgium and the Netherlands

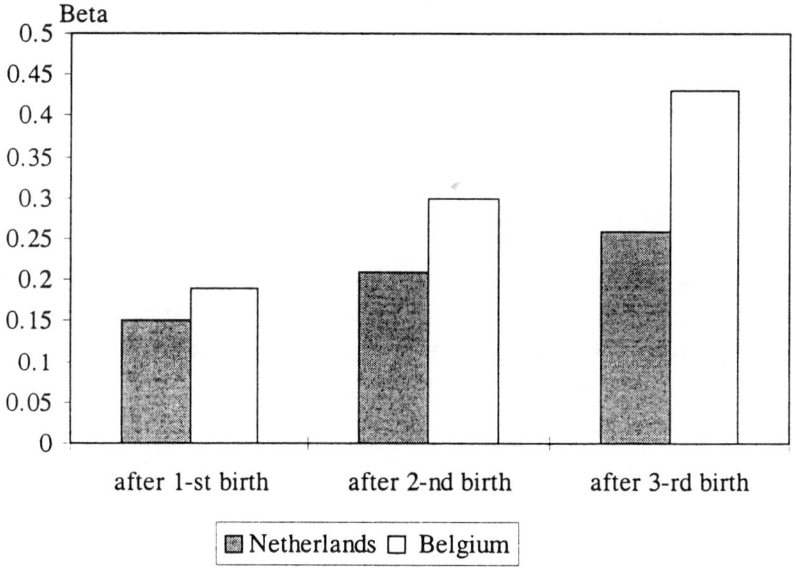

Figure 5.7. Percentage of working women, by education and parity, Belgium and the Netherlands

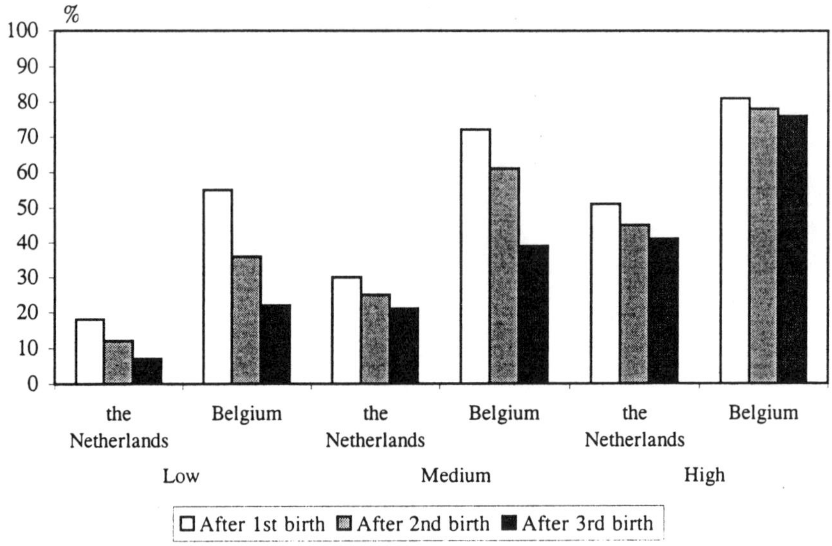

As was expected in *section 5.3.2*, the main explanatory variable for paid work by mothers is education. The higher the educational level, the higher the participation rate. This is especially true for Belgium. The effect is further enhanced in both countries for higher levels of parity (*Figure 5.6*). *Figure 5.7* illustrates that among more highly educated women parity has a small effect on labour force participation while among poorly educated women parity has a significant effect.

5.6 Conclusions

The analyses discussed in *section 5.5* reveal clear differences between Belgium and the Netherlands as far as working mothers with young children are concerned. Belgium's participation pattern can be labelled average within a European perspective. The Dutch pattern differs considerably: a relatively low percentage of working mothers and a high proportion with a part-time job. However, a catching-up effect is noted as far as the total percentage of working mothers is concerned. In Belgium, this number has risen much less sharply in recent years, although the proportion of mothers working part-time has shown a sharp rise.

Generally speaking, the analyses of the results of NEGO V and OG'93 confirm our hypothese of *section 5.3* that education has a strong impact on labour force participation. The dominant effect of education is even stronger in Belgium than in the Netherlands. More highly educated women are much more likely to work after the birth of a child than those with a lower educational level. Moreover, for every subsequent child, the rate for less well educated women drops significantly, while the participation of more highly educated women remains at nearly the same level. This is in accordance with the economic theory of the costs of children: more highly educated women have the most to lose if they give up their job. Our analyses confirm the hypothesis with respect to the effect of the mother's age when children are born: the older the mother, the more likely she is to keep her job.
For the Netherlands, in particular, it was to be expected that religious mothers would participate less in the labour market than non-religious women. This is indeed the case, although the effect is much smaller than that of education. For religious women too, the traditional household pattern is now losing ground. In Belgium, religion no longer has any influence in this respect.

References

Becker, G. (1981), *A treatise on the family*. Mass./London: Harvard University Press.

Bernhardt, E.M. (1986), Women's home attachment at first birth. *European Journal of Population,* pp. 5-29.

Blossfeld, H-P. and G. Rohwer (1993), *Family cycle and growth in women's part-time work in West Germany*, Paper presented at the EC conference on the Family Cycle and Growth of Part-Time Employment, University of Bremen.

Callens, M. (1995), Family Life Cycle and Employment in Flanders: Results from Nego V (1991). In: H. van den Brekel and F. Deven (eds.), *Population and Family in the Low Countries 1994*, Dordrecht: Kluwer Academic Publishers, pp. 81-106.

CBS (1993), Kinderopvang: gebruik en gebruikers. *Sociaal-cultureel bericht,* 11.

CBS (1994), *Relatie- en gezinsvorming in de jaren negentig*. Voorburg/Heerlen.

Commissie van de Europese Gemeenschappen (1990), *Kinderopvang en -verzorging in de Europese Gemeenschap*, 1985-1990 (special issue of "Vrouwen van Europa").

Commission of the European Communities (CEC) (1993), *Employment in Europe - 1993*, Luxembourg.

Deven, F. (1998), Belgium as a cross-road of childcare in Europe. In: JJ. Schippers et al. (Eds.), *Child care on female labour supply in the Netherlands.* Amsterdam: Thesis Publications, pp. 105-121.

European Commission Network on Childcare and other Measures to Reconcile Employment and Family Responsibilities (1996), *A Review of Services for Young Children in the European Union, 1990-1995.* Brussels, EC/DG V, Equal Opportunities Unit.

Esping-Andersen, G. (1990), *The three worlds of welfare capitalism*, Cambridge: Polity Press.

Feijter, H. de (1990), *Voorlopers bij demografische veranderingen*. NIDI Report, 22.

Groot, W. and G. Jehoel-Gijsbers (1989), *De invloed van loon en uitkering op arbeidsmarktgedrag*. The Hague, Ministerie van Sociale Zaken en Werkgelegenheid.

Gustafsson, S.S. (1991), Half the power, half the income and half the glory: the use of microeconomic theory in women's emancipation research. *The Economist*, 4, pp. 515-529.

Henkens, K., L. Meijer and J. Siegers (1993), The Labour Supply of Married and Cohabiting Women in the Netherlands, 1981-1989. *European Journal of Population*, 4, pp. 331-352.

Holderbeke F. (1991), *De onvrijwillige deeltijdse tewerkstelling in Vlaanderen*, Leuven: HIVA.

Huisman J. and E.M. Pot (1987), Nieuwe verzorgingsarrangementen; zicht op kinderlijke eenvoud. *Sociaal Maandblad Arbeid*, pp. 419-428.

Jong, A de (1995), Ontwikkelingen in de arbeidsparticipatie van moeders, *Maandstatistiek van de bevolking 32,* 11, pp. 6-18.

Jong-Gierveld, J. de and E. Beekink (1989), Veranderende waardenoriëntatie en gedrag: een vergelijking tussen twee generaties vrouwelijke academici. *Bevolking en Gezin*, 3 , pp. 53-110.

Lesthaeghe, R. and D. Meekers (1987), Demografische verschuivingen en de evolutie van waardenpatronen in de Europese Gemeenschap. *Tijdschrift voor Sociologie*, 8, pp. 129-197.

Mertens N., P. Van der Meer, J. Schippers and J. Siegers (1992), De arbeidsparticipatie van de gehuwde vrouw en de gezinsopbouw: gedragen Nederlandse vrouwen zich anders dan Vlaamse vrouwen? *Bevolking en Gezin*, 3, pp. 105-129.

Ministerie van WVC (1992), *Stimuleringsbeleid Kinderopvang 1990-1993*.

Ministerie van Tewerkstelling en Arbeid (1994), *De arbeidsmarkt in België: werkgelegenheid en werkloosheid*, Brussels.

Mott, F.L. and D. Shapiro (1983), Complementarity of work and fertility among young American mothers. *Population Studies 37*, pp. 239-252.

Pauwels K., W. Van Dongen, L. Deschamps and E. Bosman (1988), De arbeidsparticipatie van de vrouw en de gezinsopbouw, *Bevolking en Gezin*, 3, pp. 237-248.

Plantenga, J. and A. van Doorne-Huiskens (1993), Verschillen in arbeidsmarktposities van vrouwen in Europa. *Tijdschrift voor Arbeidsvraagstukken*, pp. 51-62.

Pott-Buter, H.A. (1993), *Facts and Fairy Tales about Female Labor Family and Fertility. A Seven-Country Comparison. 1850-1990*. Amsterdam: Amsterdam University Press.

Pott-Buter, H.A. (1994), De bijzondere arbeidsmarktpositie van Nederlandse vrouwen. *Economische Statistische Berichten 78* (no. 3958), pp. 352-356.

Ramioul, M. (1993), Two-speed flexibility and the position of females on the labour market in Flanders. In: Beets et al. (eds.), *Population and Family in the Low Countries 1992*: Family and Labour, Amsterdam/Lisse: Swets & Zeitlinger, pp. 169-193.

SCP (1993), *Sociale atlas van de vrouw*, part 2. Rijswijk.

Siegers, J. (1985), *Arbeidsaanbod en kindertal, een micro-economische analyse*. Thesis. Groningen: Rijksuniversiteit.

Sperber, B.M., M. Fishbein and I. Ajzen (1980), Predicting and understanding women's occupational orientations: factors underlying choice intentions. In: I. Ajzen and M. Fishbein (eds.), *Understanding attitudes and predicting social behaviour*. New Jersey: Prentice Hall.

Triest, M. (1993), De arbeidsmarktposities van vrouwen in België en de rol van de verzorgingsstaat. In: *Tijdschrift voor Arbeidsvraagstukken*, 9, pp. 63-65.

Tweede Kamer der Staten Generaal, (1994), *Gelijke behandeling deeltijd/voltijd*. Vergaderjaar 1994-1995, 24020, no. 1. The Hague.

Vendrik, M. (1993), *Collective habits and social norms*. Maastricht: Universitaire Pers Maastricht.

Vendrik, M. (1994), Invloed van sociale normen. In: *Economisch Statistische Berichten*, 78 (no. 3958), pp. 369-372.

Vermunt, J.K. (1991), Leefstijl en demografisch gedrag: een toepassing van een latente-klasse analyse. In: *Maandstatistiek van de bevolking*, 39, 11, pp. 13-25.

Vries, R.F. de (1993), Opleiding en verschillen in arbeidsmarktparticipatie en vruchtbaarheidsgedrag van vrouwen. *Bevolking en Gezin*, 1, pp. 45-63.

Walle, F. van de (1980), Education and the demographic transition in Switzerland. In: *Demography*, 6, 3, pp. 463-472.

Wiebrens, C.J. (1981), *Inkomen en Rondkomen*. The Hague: Sociaal Cultureel Planbureau.

6. SUMMARY AND DISCUSSION

Joop de Beer, Martine Corijn and Fred Deven

In comparing family and fertility behaviour between European countries, some authors emphasise the similarity of trends across countries, whereas others argue that even though there are remarkable similarities, important inter-country differences persist. Most European countries have witnessed a postponement of marriage and parenthood and an increase in unmarried cohabitation and extramarital fertility. Nevertheless there still exist important differences in demographic behaviour across European countries. For example, the level of fertility in Southern Europe is considerably lower than in Northern Europe, whereas consensual unions are much more popular in Northern countries than in the South. The contrast between developments in the same direction on the one hand and still existing differences on the other raises the question whether converging trends will be predominant or whether inter-country differences will persist. The concept of the Second Demographic Transition, introduced by Lesthaeghe and Van de Kaa (1986) suggest that European countries experience one common transition process. This implies that differences across European countries are temporary. Inter-country differences are due to the fact that countries are in a different stage of the transition process. This may be caused by differences in the timing of the onset of the process or differences in the rate of change. In the course of the process inter-country differences will decline or possibly even disappear. One alternative interpretation of the transition process is that even though similar trends have been observed in many countries, between-country differences in family and fertility behaviour will not disappear due to differences in the economic, institutional and cultural context (e.g. Kuijsten, 1996). During the last decades in all Western European countries incomes have risen, economic structures have changed, labour force participation of women has risen, the participation

J. de Beer and F. Deven (eds.), Diversity in Family Formation, 115–130.

in education has increased, the authority of normative institutions has eroded, and individualisation has lead to more freedom of individuals to organise their own life. These changes have affected the transition from youth to adulthood (Liefbroer, 1999). Nevertheless important economic and cultural differences still exist across European countries. For example, the female labour force participation rate in Sweden is about twice that in Italy. Per capita GNP in Northern and Western Europe is about fifty percent higher than in Portugal and Greece. In Nordic countries child care facilities and parental leave are more widespread than in other parts of Europe (Moss & Deven, 1999). In Southern Europe family values are more traditional than in Northern Europe. Differences in the economic and social structure as well as differences in value patterns across European countries may explain differences in family formation processes. Hofstede (1981) claims that cultural differences between European countries are very stable through time. Even though there are global trends that affect all countries (e.g. globalisation, increasing communication, technological developments, changes in the physical environment), the reactions of people to these global changes differ due to durable cultural differences. According to Hofstede there is only a convergence of superficial aspects of culture (e.g. consumption patterns, amusement), but not of the fundamental values. This would imply that differences in family formation behaviour across European countries are likely to persist.

The aim of this book is to examine changes in the start of the family formation process. Analysing differences between many countries on an aggregate level may lead to results that are difficult to interpret. First, differences at the aggregate level may be caused by both differences in the composition of the population and by micro-level differences. Second, if countries differ in many aspects, it is difficult to identify the causes of differences in demographic behaviour, as the differences may be attributed to many sources. Usually comparative studies focus on differences between Northern and Southern European countries. The societal context in these countries differs so widely that it is difficult to interpret demographic differences. A comparison of differences in changes in family formation and fertility behaviour between Belgium and the Netherlands is interesting because even though the economic and cultural differences between these countries are relatively small there is one important difference: Belgium is predominantly Catholic, whereas the Netherlands has about equal proportions of Catholics and Protestants. If the Second Demographic Transition implies that there is one common pattern of change in different European countries and that differences across countries are due to the fact that countries are in a different stage of the transition process, and if it is assumed that the transition process started earlier in Protestant countries than in Catholic countries, one would expect that the Netherlands are in a further stage of the transition process than Belgium. Thus an in-depth comparison of changes in family formation and fertility behaviour between Belgium and the Netherlands may give us more insight in the question whether there is one common transition process.

Van de Kaa (1997) identifies three major shifts in fertility and family behaviour since the 1960s: (1) changes in contraceptive behaviour; (2) changes in the level and pattern of fertility; (3) changes in the timing, type, frequency and stability of unions. Actually, he distinguishes a fourth shift, i.e. changes in the types of family patterns, but this shift can be regarded as the result of the other three shifts rather than as a separate source of demographic change. *Chapters 2 to 5* compare the three major shifts in family and fertility behaviour in Belgium and the Netherlands. The analysis focuses on the early stage of the life cycle. For this reason, the start of the family formation process is analysed rather than the dissolution of partnerships. *Chapter 2* analyses contraceptive behaviour, *Chapter 3* studies the choice of living arrangement after leaving the parental home, *Chapter 4* examines changes in the timing and level of fertility, and *Chapter 5* pays special attention to the relationship between fertility and female labour force participation.

On the basis of the empirical findings of *Chapters 2 to 5*, the present chapter attempts to understand some of the similarities and differences in trends between Belgium and the Netherlands by referring to differences in the sociocultural environment and in welfare policy measures. Rather than inferring causality, however, a number of associations will be described to raise hypotheses which may be useful for further research.

6.1 Summing up: the position of the Netherlands and Belgium in a demographic transition process

The concept of the second demographic transition refers to important changes in fertility and family behaviour, such as an increase in unmarried cohabitation, the postponement of marriage and parenthood and an increase in childlessness (Lesthaeghe & Van de Kaa, 1986). The comparison of Fertility and Family Survey-data in the Netherlands and in Belgium brings us to the core question of whether there is one common explanation for differences between countries in the three types of fertility and family behaviour under study. Can differences between Belgium and the Netherlands be explained by differences in the stage of the second demographic transition?

6.1.1 Contraceptive behaviour

The contraceptive transition in Belgium resembled that of Southern European countries (slower rate of change with a slow decline in the practice of withdrawal and/or the rhythm method, later acceptance of hormonal, intra-uterine and surgical contraception and low use of barrier methods). The transition in the Netherlands was more closely comparable to the transition characteristic of North-Western Europe, where the transition occurred very early and barrier methods provided an important link in the transition from 'traditional' to 'modern' methods.

In the early 1980s, the contraceptive profiles of Belgium and the Netherlands already showed a high level of similarity. Contraceptive methods were applied by nearly all fecund women who were sexually active and who were not and did not want to become pregnant. Mainly modern methods were used. Relatively more Dutch women used surgical contraception.
Changes were also similar in both countries. The proportion of women who used no fertility-regulating method remained unchanged, except among 21-25 year-olds, where the percentage of non-users decreased. A rise in the use of hormonal contraception was observed among all age groups and the use of the IUD declined. In the Netherlands, however, the use of the condom increased, although mainly among 31-37 year-olds, compared to Belgium, where it remained almost the same. In Belgium, withdrawal and/or periodic abstinence continued to decrease, a trend already observed since the 1960s.

During the nineteen-eighties, surgical contraception declined significantly in the Netherlands, especially among women. A trend towards delaying sterilisation is observed from the cohort 1954-56 onwards, probably connected to the postponement of childbearing. In the early 1990s, the percentage of sterilised partners of women aged 31-37 was three times that of sterilised women in that age group. In Belgium too, surgical contraception increased sharply among 31-37 year-old men, although the proportion of women still exceeds that of men.

Abortions fell among 21-44 year-old Dutch women from 6.2‰ in 1980 to 5.6‰ in 1992. In Belgium too, there was probably a decline (6‰ in 1993). In the early nineteen-nineties, abortion rates in the Low Countries are low compared to other European countries. Multivariate analyses for cohorts born since 1950 reveal only a small influence in the Netherlands and none in Belgium of social characteristics such as education or frequency of church attendance (de Graaf & Lodewijckx, *Chapter 2*). The woman's age remains the most important differentiating variable for contraceptive choice, which obviously relates to the phase of family formation which differs according to the woman's educational level. Moreover, Roman Catholic women who attend church regularly most often use 'traditional' methods.

The Netherlands and Belgium also differ in their timing of the start of a woman's fertility career (especially the first birth). Their contraceptive pattern, however, is similar, as Belgium has caught up with the very effective profile of the Netherlands.

6.1.2 Choice of living arrangement after leaving the parental home

There is a strong country-specific difference in the age at which young adults leave their parental home. In both countries, a postponement can be discerned in the timing of leaving the parental home over the cohorts born since 1950, especially for the youngest male cohort of 1961-65. However, the general process of leaving the parental home is much faster in the Netherlands than in Belgium. In the youngest cohort, for example, 55% of Dutch women (Dutch men, 31%) have left the parental home by the age of 20, compared to approximately 33% of Belgian women (Belgian men, 12%).
Moreover, the kind of living arrangement chosen is quite country-specific. In the Netherlands, marriage is no longer the main route for leaving the parental home, in contrast to Belgium, although other pathways are gaining in popularity.
In both countries, albeit at a different tempo, the postponement of leaving home in general coincides with the postponement of leaving home through marriage. The proportion of young adults leaving home to marry before the age of 25 decreased in Belgium by about 20% and by about 27% in the Netherlands. The decline in the marriage risk across the cohorts is much higher in the Netherlands than in Belgium.
Young adults in Belgium have a much lower risk of flying the nest to cohabit than in the Netherlands. This choice, however, has increased in popularity and occurs at younger ages. Country-specific differences in leaving home to cohabit were at a maximum in the Netherlands for the cohort 1956-60. In Belgium, however, the popularity of unmarried cohabitation has increased to an extent that the youngest cohort (1961-65) is catching up with the oldest Dutch cohort (1951-55). Young adults in Belgium have a much lower risk of leaving home when single than in the Netherlands (still 2.6 times higher

among the youngest female cohort) where this transition remains more popular than in Belgium; it did not change much across the birth cohorts studied here. Country-specific differences are absent for men. The different timing for leaving the parental home and the different pathways chosen at that time, result in the much higher proportion of young adults living or having lived an unmarried cohabitation and in a much higher age for first marriage in the Netherlands.

With regard to the onset of family formation behaviour, the developments of the 1970s and 1980s show a pattern of change in the same direction for both countries: postponement of the age for leaving the parental home and at first marriage and the increased popularity of non-traditional routes for leaving the parental home, especially in the Netherlands. There is, however, a difference in the onset of these changes and a strong time lag in the level of these trends between the two countries. The Dutch cohort of 1951-55 had a higher risk of leaving home by either route than the same Belgian cohort. With regard to the timing and the route for leaving the parental home, the Belgian cohort born in 1951-55 resembles the Dutch cohorts born in 1961-65. This 'lagging behind' of about ten birth-cohort years raises the question of whether there is only a difference in tempo or a difference with regard to a possible saturation level as well. With regard to the start of family formation behaviour, the Netherlands can be considered more advanced in the transition process and as having a more differentiated family system, since the parental home is left earlier in favour of living in other living arrangements before marriage.

The multivariate analysis of the timing and the routes out of the parental home in the Netherlands and in Belgium revealed significant country-specific determinants, even after controlling for resources in the parental home (e.g. education and religion) (Corijn and Manting, *Chapter 3*). Religious parents only moderately stimulate the process of leaving the parental home through marriage but significantly slow down this transition by unmarried cohabitation, particularly for Belgian women. The parental religious affiliation plays no role at all in the Netherlands for people leaving home as single, but has some impact in Belgium where its popularity is still low. The intellectual climate in the parental home has a strong influence on the home-leaving behaviour of the adolescents. Having more highly educated parents reduces the risks of leaving the parental home through marriage by about 50%, similarly in both countries. It strongly increases the risks leaving home when single, but it does not influence the pathway of leaving home through unmarried cohabitation.

Liefbroer et al. (1996) found hardly any impact among males, whereas the parental educational level did have an impact among females. Belgian females with highly educated parents had rates for entering into unmarried cohabitation that were twice as high as females whose parents had lower levels of education. Such differences were much smaller among Dutch females and went in the opposite direction.

6.1.3 Fertility

Although young adults in the Netherlands leave their parental home at younger ages than in Belgium, they have their children when they are older. The mean age of women when the first child is born is about one year higher in the Netherlands than in Belgium, a difference which increased during the 1980s. Whereas the difference between countries of the age for childbirth is increasing, the average number of children per woman has been decreasing. For Dutch women born in 1935, the average family size was about 2.5, compared to 2.3 for Belgian women. This difference between countries has almost disappeared for women born in 1950; it is now about 1.9 (de Jong and Lodewijckx, *Chapter 4*).

In 1993, 16% of Dutch women born between 1951-1955 were still childless, while 12% of Belgian women born in the same period were still childless in 1991. There is a positive relationship between childlessness and the level of educational attainment. The impact of education on childlessness is larger in the Netherlands than in Belgium. For birth cohort 1951-1955, the difference between women with high and low levels of educational attainment is 11 percentage points in the Netherlands and 7 in Belgium. For younger birth cohorts, there is a strong difference in childlessness between high and low educational levels. This difference is mainly caused by differences in timing. Since highly educated women have postponed childbearing, the percentage of childlessness among highly educated women aged 25 to 30 years is relatively high. However, there is hardly any difference in expected childlessness between educational levels. The educational attainment appears to have hardly any influence on the desire to have children. The impact of education is mainly a matter of timing, but for some women, a postponement of childbearing may lead to permanent childlessness.

The average family size for women born between 1951-1955 is 1.8 children in both countries. The difference by educational level is not the same in Belgium and the Netherlands. Belgian women with an average level of educational attainment born between 1951-1955 have 0.1 fewer children than women with low and high educational levels. Dutch women with a high level of educational attainment have 0.25 fewer children than women with an average educational level and 0.40 fewer children than women with a low level of education. The lower fertility of highly educated Dutch women is usually related to difficulties in combining motherhood with labour force participation. In Belgium, an income effect may be at play, since highly educated women have more financial resources for raising children than women with an average educational level whereas women with poor education on average tend to become full-time housewives and mothers.

6.1.4 Female labour force participation

The labour force participation of women and the combination of female labour force participation and motherhood prove to be quite different in the Netherlands and Belgium (Callens, van Hoorn and de Jong, *Chapter 5*).

As in other countries in the European Union, the activity rate of 25-49 year-old women has risen sharply in recent decades. In the early 1960s, female activity profiles in both countries showed the same basic pattern: a curve with one (high) peak for 20-25 years-old and falling activity rates for the older age groups, reflecting a situation in which women stop working following their marriage and/or when they become mothers. By contrast, even though the basic pattern in both countries was similar, the activity rate of older age groups (e.g. 30-34 year old women) was much lower (16%) in the Netherlands than in Belgium (33%). In the early 1990s, some of the differences between the two countries were reduced. A striking difference remains the high level (59%) of part-time employment among Dutch women, compared with an overall percentage of 30% among Belgian women in 1991, which posits Belgium more to the centre among Member States of the European Union (Eurostat, 1993, Table 34).

The differing interdependence between countries between the female labour force participation career and the motherhood career can be described as follows. Before the birth of the first child, there are few differences between Dutch and Belgian patterns of female labour force participation as nearly all young women are full-time employed during this stage in their life cycle. After the birth of the first child, the Dutch pattern differs considerably, with an overall low percentage of working mothers, to a large extent on a part-time basis. Belgium witnesses a more gradual decline in the labour force participation of mothers to just under 50% after the birth of the third child.

To the extent that the functional independence between female labour force participation and motherhood are considered to express more 'modern' behaviour, Belgium is more 'advanced' in the second demographic transition.

The different activity profile for women and the different link between the activity profile and the number of children is reflected in the supply of childcare facilities. In this respect, Belgium and the Netherlands occupy opposite positions in Europe. Only Denmark scores higher than Belgium among the 12 EU Member States for the percentage of publicly-funded services for children under three (European Commission Network on Childcare, 1996: Figure 5.6). The Netherlands has a low score, since only one quarter of working women with children under four years of age uses external childcare (day-care centres or registered childminder). In Belgium, one quarter of children under the age 3 attend day-care centres and one quarter go to childminders.

The impact of the women's educational level is only noticeable following the birth of the first child. Highly educated mothers in both countries continue to work significantly more and are less likely to work part-time. This effect becomes stronger the larger the family becomes. The differential impact of educational level on the labour force participation pattern, related to the family formation process, proves to be much stronger in Belgium than in the Netherlands. Can the stronger differential impact of educational level in Belgium be understood by the more 'advanced' supply of childcare services and/or regulations (e.g. career break system) for combining labour force participation with motherhood?

6.2 General discussion

Throughout *Chapters 2 to 5*, several types of fertility and family behaviour were analysed, mainly based on Fertility and Family Survey data in Belgium (1991-92) and the Netherlands (1993). Considering the use of fertility regulating methods, the choice of living arrangement upon leaving the parental home, the expected and actual number of children of women and of mothers, as well as the combination of motherhood and labour force participation, it is difficult to define in a simple way the position of both countries with respect to the onset, rate, intensity and saturation level of the demographic transition process.

The global pattern of results with regard to these types of demographic behaviour indicates that the two countries are at different stages of the transition process. The order of their position, however, is dependent on the topic under study. For one type of behaviour, the Netherlands seems to be at a more advanced stage than Belgium (choice of first living arrangement), whereas for another type of behaviour, the opposite applies (labour force participation of mothers) and, for a third type of behaviour, both countries seem to be at the same stage (contraceptive practice). The rate of some of these demographic changes suggests a different onset and a time lag of about ten cohort years; but this does not apply to all types of change. The rate of some changes reflects differences between countries, whereas the level of the changes suggests that the saturation points for some developments may not turn out to be the same. The empirical results summed up in *section 6.1* suggest that the different types of change in family and fertility behaviour cannot simply be interpreted in terms of one model of the second demographic transition. In general, it is documented that the rate at which different populations in Europe have adopted specific patterns of demographic behaviour has differed greatly and continues to reflect clear differences (Coleman, 1996; van de Kaa, 1999; Leridon, 1999).

This section therefore aims to check whether differences in some aspects of fertility and family behaviour reflect similar or different underlying processes. Firstly, some consideration is given to the question of whether the composition of the population of each country differs with regard to characteristics that are relevant for (changes in) demographic behaviour.

Looking for factors which influence the diffusion of demographic changes, Lesthaeghe (1991) checked to what extent national leads and lags were conditioned or mediated by cultural factors, by historical features and by economic factors, such as the structural changes affecting the economic autonomy of women. He finds, at the macro-level, that political aspects associated with individual autonomy and female emancipation are indispensable ingredients. It implies that explanations which rely solely on either ideational changes or on structural-economic factors are non-redundant, yet insufficient. The historical role of Protestantism accounts for both a greater political emphasis on individual autonomy and for a more rapid development of female economic autonomy.
Whereas Belgium is predominantly Roman Catholic, the Netherlands has about equal numbers of Protestants and Roman Catholics. Data from the European Values Study reveal that, despite the major socio-cultural similarities between the Netherlands and Belgium, there are particular differences as

several results point to the more secularised character of the Netherlands (Halman, 1991). If non-religious people are considered forerunners for some types of demographic behaviour, the Netherlands can obviously be expected to be a country which is further ahead of a general trend. The probable impact of Protestantism is another argument in this respect.

There seem to be no strong compositional differences between countries with respect to education. Our FFS data show a similar proportion of respondents with a high level of education (Belgian, 33% and Dutch, 26%) as well as of respondents with highly educated parents (about 14%). This provides no basis for expecting more 'modern' fertility and family behaviour in either of the Low Countries. The link between educational level as such and the degree of female labour force participation differs in both countries.

Based on the population composition with regard to these two characteristics, no simple prediction can be made of the potential of forerunners or innovators within each country. Another argument for a lack of any compositional effect can be derived from multivariate analyses. Liefbroer et al. (1996) found country-specific differences between Belgium and the Netherlands with regard to the influence of some determinants on union and family formation behaviour, which remained after controls for the compositional differences of factors such as parental background, religiosity, educational level and activity status.

With respect to the timing and the route for leaving the parental home we tend to conclude that the family system is more differentiated in the Netherlands, since less traditional living arrangements such as unmarried cohabitation and living alone are more prevalent. The trend towards postponing the timing of leaving the parental home started somewhat earlier as well. Some structural differences and policy measures between both countries may be considered. For example, Dutch students living outside the parental home were, until recently, entitled to a state scholarship. They can even obtain a supplementary loan if their parents' income is modest. Moreover, young Dutch adults may receive a subsidy if the rent for their accommodation exceeds their means of subsistence. Such generous conditions, which did not prevail in Belgium during the same period, may partly explain the choice of less traditional living arrangements, such as living alone.
The assumption that the transition process is at a more advanced stage if differences between social groups become smaller is not carried by all the results related to leaving the parental home. In this domain, the transition in Belgium seems to be at an earlier stage and further developments may be

expected. In view of some important differences related to the parents' religious affiliation, some room remains for further developments in the Netherlands (e.g. unmarried cohabitation). Differences between countries are expected to narrow down, but some may be more permanent. The hypothesis that social differences are stronger provided the behaviour is rather uncommon (e.g. leaving home while still single) is only partially supported by our data.

The Netherlands had already achieved a quasi-perfect pattern of fertility regulating behaviour by the early 1980s. About a decade later, the same can be claimed for Belgium. In the former country, the earlier adaptation of new legislation as well as the development of good medical and psycho-social services certainly did contribute to this outcome. Given the disappearance of differences between countries, those between social groups disappeared completely in Belgium, but remained to some extent in the Netherlands. The remaining minor impact of religion and education in the Netherlands (e.g. the use of somewhat more 'traditional' methods) may be understood as a kind of polarisation effect occurring at the onset and at the end of a transition process.

For young generations of women the percentage of childlessness is higher in the Netherlands than in Belgium. To an important extent this may be explained by differences in the postponement of fertility. This is suggested by the fact that the percentage of young women expecting to remain childless hardly differs between both countries; about ten percent of young women do not expect to have children. However, one should be careful in interpreting these figures as expectations may not be realised. Due to several causes, such as infecundity, divorce and changed preferences, the ultimate level of childlessness will probably exceed expectations.
The effect of the level of educational attainment on observed childlessness is higher in the Netherlands than in Belgium. This does not lead to an unambiguous conclusion about the stage of the Second Demographic Transition. One possible interpretation is that Belgium is in an earlier stage of the transition process than the Netherlands. In the first stage of the transition process differences between social categories tend to widen, as vanguard groups introduce new types of behaviour that are not yet adopted by other groups. Only after some years do other social categories follow their example. Thus in later stages of the transition process differences between social categories become smaller. If Belgium is in an earlier stage of the transition to higher levels of childlessness than the Netherlands the differences in childlessness between education categories may increase in the future. An alternative in-

terpretation, however, is that Belgium is in a further stage of the transition which would imply that the differences between social groups will decline. As regards the labour force participation pattern of mothers, the inter-country differences are pronounced but cannot be understood in a simple way. Belgium has a higher female activity rate. Differences between the two countries have diminished but are still strong. Part-time work increased in Belgium but is not as popular as in the Netherlands. The labour force participation pattern of women changes in Belgium between the second and the third child; in the Netherlands this already happens following the arrival of the first child.

Despite the lower activity rate in the Netherlands, the differences between groups with respect to education are less marked than in Belgium. The more uncommon behaviour of being a (full-time) working mother in the Netherlands is affected by educational level, but to a lesser degree than in Belgium. The more common behaviour of being a working mother in Belgium is strongly affected by women's educational level. These results do not fit in with the idea that differences between groups disappear as behaviour becomes more common. The parity-specific activity rate of less well educated mothers in Belgium remains higher compared to that of highly educated Dutch women.

The minor influence of religion on the activity rate of women in the Netherlands and the absence of such an influence in Belgium also remains hard to interpret. In the more secularised Netherlands, the polarisation effect of the 'last religious people' can be invoked. In less secularised Belgium, moral ethics seems to have no impact on the labour force participation pattern of women.

The sharper drop in the female labour force participation rate in the Netherlands following the birth of the first child suggests that Dutch women (and their partners, if any) value motherhood in a different way and/or that the combination of parenthood and labour force participation is more difficult in the Netherlands. In a study of the Population Policy Acceptance research data, it became clear that Belgian and Dutch women have different preferences with regard to the combination of work and family (Van Peer & Moors, 1996). Belgian and Dutch women to the same extent opt for an identical and preferred combination: part-time work and caring for one or more children (47%). The second best combination preferred by Belgian women is a full-time job and caring for one or more children (38%); a combination that is the choice of only 8% of Dutch women. The second best combination

preferred by the latter is "temporarily or permanently no work if there are children" (36%); a combination that is the choice of only 10% of Belgian women.
This raises the question of to what extent the differences in the female labour force participation rate in the early 1990s can be understood or explained by the lower availability of childcare facilities in the Netherlands. The sharper drop in the activity rate of Dutch women following the transition into motherhood invokes the more difficult combination of labour force participation and motherhood in the Netherlands. In both countries, a higher level of educational attainment implies a higher activity rate, which can imply that one is more capable of affording childcare facilities. However, one may question whether income alone determines the possibility of affording childcare services in addition to other facilities (e.g. the career break system) making it somewhat easier to combine labour force participation and motherhood.
It may be noted that the supply of childcare facilities differs quite markedly between Belgium and the Netherlands. Within the context of the Member States of the European Union, Belgium has quite a high percentage of places for children under three, certainly compared with the Netherlands (European Commission Network on Childcare, 1996).
Another plausible hypothesis can be found in differences between policy measures. In the Netherlands, both government policy (e.g. the level of the minimum wage and of social security benefits) and the negotiation policy of the trade unions used to be aimed at guaranteeing income levels that were high enough to support a whole family. Hence, average income has been relatively high in the Netherlands. In addition, there have been many policy measures to support low-income families. One important example is the housing policy. The Dutch government has spent large amounts of subsidies on housing. For instance, a subsidy is available for families whose rent for accommodation is relatively high compared to their family income. Hence, it is possible to hypothesise that many women felt no need to find a paid job in order to raise the family income, particularly because this type of subsidy is reduced if women are earning their own income.

Differences in family formation and fertility behaviour between Belgium and the Netherlands cannot simply be explained by assuming that both countries are at a different stage of one common demographic transition process. Even though the economic and cultural differences between Belgium and the Netherlands are relatively small there are important differences in family formation behaviour. These differences cannot simply be explained by the fact that Belgium is predominantly Catholic and that as a consequence Belgium follows the same transition process as the Netherlands with some time lag. If even these two resembling, neighbouring countries do not experience the same transition process, it will be less likely still that other European countries go through one common process. Even though changes in demographic behaviour across Europe have been characterised by developments in similar directions, there is no reason to expect the end of diversity in family formation and fertility behaviour in Europe.

References

Blossfeld H.P. (1995), The new role of women. Family formation in modern societies. Boulder: Westview Press.

Callens, M., van Hoorn, W. and A. de Jong (this volume). *Labour force participation of mothers.*

EC/DG V (1995), La situation démographique dans l'Union européenne. Report 1994. Brussels/Luxembourg, DG V - COM (94) 595.

Coleman D. (1996), New Patterns and Trends in European Fertility: International and subnational Comparisons. In: D. Coleman (ed.), Europe's Population in the 1990s. Oxford University Press. pp. 1-61

Corijn, M. and J. de Beer (1996). Family Formation and Fertility in Belgium and the Netherlands. In: Proceedings of the European Population Conference 1995. Milan: Franco Angeli, volume 2. pp. 31-47

Corijn, M. and D. Manting (this volume). *The choice of living arrangement after leaving the parental home.*

European Commission Network on Childcare and other Measures to Reconcile Employment and Family Responsibilities (1996), *A Review of Services for Young Children in the European Union, 1990-1995.* Brussels: EC/DG V, Equal Opportunities Unit.

De Feijter, H. (1991). *Voorlopers bij demografische veranderingen* (Forerunners in demographic changes). The Hague: NIDI report 22.

De Graaf A. and E. Lodewijckx (this volume). *Fertility regulation.*

De Jong, A. and E. Lodewijckx (this volume). *Fertility.*

Halman, L. (1991), Waarden in de Westerse wereld. Tilburg: Tilburg University Press.

Hofstede, G. (1981), *Culture's consequences. International differences in work-related values.* London: Sage Publications.

Kuijsten, A.C. (1996), Changing family patterns in Europe: A case of divergence? *European Population Studies* 12, 115-143.

Leridon, H. (1999), *Les nouveaux modes de planification de la famille en Europe European Populations. Unity in Diversity.* Dordrecht/London: Kluwer Academic Publ. pp. 51-76 (European Studies of Population, 6).

Lesthaeghe, R. (1991), The second demographic transition in Western Countries: an interpretation. Brussels: IPD Working paper.

Lesthaeghe, R. and D.J. van de Kaa (1986), Twee demografische transities? *Mens en Maatschappij,* 61, pp. 9-24.

Lesthaeghe, R. and G. Moors (1995), Living Arrangements, Socio-economic Position, and Values among Young Adults: a Pattern Description for Belgium, France, the Netherlands and West Germany, 1990). In: H. van den Brekel and F. Deven (eds.), *Population and Family in the Low Countries 1994. Selected Current Issues,* Dordrecht/London: Kluwer Academic Publ. pp. 1-56.(European Studies of Population, 2).

Liefbroer, A. (1999), From youth to adulthood: understanding changing patterns of family formation from a life course perspective (pp. 53-85). In: L. van Wissen and P.Dykstra (eds.), *Population Issues. An Interdisciplinary Focus*. New York: Kluwer-Academic/-Plenum Publishers.

Liefbroer, A.C., M. Corijn and J. de Jong-Gierveld (1996), Similarity and Diversity in the Onset of Family Formation in the Low Countries. Brussels: CBGS Document, 3.

Moss, P. and F. Deven (eds.) (1999), *Parental Leave: Progress or Pitfall? Research and Policy Issues in Europe.* The Hague/Brussels: NIDI/CBGS Publications: vol. 35.

Van de Kaa, D.J. (1997), Options and sequences. Europe's demographic patterns. Nethur Demography Paper no. 39.

Van de Kaa, D.J. (1999), Europe and its population: the long view. *European Populations. Unity in Diversity.* Dordrecht/London: Kluwer Academic Publ. pp. 1-49 (European Studies of Population, 6).

Van Peer, C. and H.G. Moors (1996), Perceived Obstacles to Fertility and the Evaluation of Family Policies: Opinions in Flanders and in the Netherlands. In: H. van den Brekel and F. Deven (eds.), *Population and Family in the Low Countries 1995. Selected Current Issues,* Dordrecht/London: Kluwer Academic Publ. pp. 41-66 (European Studies of Population, 4).

7. TECHNICAL APPENDIX
Information on the Belgian and Dutch Fertility and Family Surveys

Arie de Graaf and Edith Lodewijckx

7.1 Introduction

This Technical Appendix mainly includes more detailed information on the Belgian and Dutch Fertility and Family Surveys (sampling, field work, (non-)response). It draws heavily on the materials prepared as Standard Country Reports for the UN/ECE project (see Latten & de Graaf, 1997; Lodewijckx, 1999).

Moreover, as announced in *Chapters 4 and 5*, it also provides more information on the MCA technique.

7.2 The Belgian survey (NEGO-V)

The samples

CBGS's 5th fertility and family survey (NEGO V) consists of two investigations, one in the Flemish Region, the other in the Brussels Capital Region, which are mainly typified by a partially different sample composition. The following samples were constituted:

a) 2 independent samples for the Flemish Region: approximately 3,000 women and 2,000 men of Belgian nationality, regardless of civil status and born during the period 1951-1970;

J. de Beer and F. Deven (eds.), Diversity in Family Formation, 131–139.

b) 8 independent samples for the Brussels Capital Region: birth cohorts 1951-1970, regardless of civil status and from the following sub-groups:
- French-speaking Belgians (400 men and 400 women)
- Dutch-speaking Belgians (400 men and 400 women)
- Other Europeans (400 men and 400 women)
- Moroccans (400 women)
- Turks (400 women).

Non-Belgian nationalities were excluded from the samples for the Flemish Region on the basis of their small numbers within the population (< 5%), and because of the fact that an inter-university research team had, in parallel with NEGO V, conducted a fertility survey among Muslim immigrants in which the NEGO V team was also represented. The sample composition specific to the Brussels population and the policy concerns regarding the immigrant question required the inclusion of ethnic variety as a basic criterion for the composition of the Brussels sample.

A two-stage cluster sampling design was utilised in the Flemish Region. In the initial stage, municipalities were selected from various socio-economic strata. In each selected municipality, individuals were selected at random. A total of 2,975 women and 1,989 men were selected to take part in the survey (Callens, 1995).

The sampling design for the Brussels Capital Region was disproportional. It consisted of eight independent samples of equal size (n = 400). The 19 municipalities of the Brussels Capital Region form equal separate strata in each sample, thus overcoming the geographical clustering of socio-economically homogenous groups. Direct, simple random sampling of individuals was applied in each of the 19 municipalities of Brussels (Daelemans & Callens, 1994).

Thanks to the availability of NEGO V data for both the Flemish Region and the Brussels Capital Region, it is possible to study the Dutch-speaking population of Belgium, or so-called "Flemish Community". Four samples are combined in this study: 1) Belgian women living in the Flemish Region; 2) Belgian men living in the Flemish Region; 3) Dutch-speaking Belgian women living in the Brussels Capital Region; and 4) Dutch-speaking Belgian men living in the Brussels Capital Region. The analyses had to be weighted as a consequence of the sampling design (Lodewijckx, 1996). This report applies weighting by region.

Collection of data

The NEGO V survey applied two paper questionnaires:
a) the questionnaire that CBGS prepared for ECE's FFS project (Cliquet, 1987; Cliquet et al., 1992), used in a face-to-face interview at the respondent's home. Respondents were questioned by interviewers of the same gender. Interviewers were recruited, instructed and counselled by CBGS staff. All interviewers attended a one-day training course before starting the fieldwork. The questionnaires were checked by CBGS. This included careful examination and - where necessary - return to the interviewer for further explanation. With the NEGO V fieldwork being planned for 1991, there was no time left to await the final version of the questionnaire as proposed by the ECE. The structure of this questionnaire also departs rather noticeably from the standard FFS questionnaire, but most SRF variables were constructed (Lodewijckx, 1996);
b) a nationally adapted version of the Population Policy Acceptance (PPA) survey questionnaire (Moors & Palomba, 1989), handed by the interviewer to the respondent with the request that it be completed after the interview and mailed to CBGS.

The survey in the Flemish Region was carried out between April and October 1991. About three-quarters of the fieldwork was completed in the first three months (Callens, 1995). The survey of the Dutch-speaking Belgians in the Brussels Capital Region was carried out in 1992. About 80% of the interviews were held before July 1992 (Daelemans & Callens, 1994).

Sample bias and non-response

Table B.1 presents, for the Flemish Region, the distribution of the universe, the target sample (panel b), the sample before substitution (panel c), the non-response rate (panel d) and the sample after substitution (panel e), by sex, birth cohort and marital status. Out of the 2,975 women selected for the survey, 887 and 670 of the 1,989 men selected were not interviewed; in other words, the non-response rate is 29.8% for women and 33.7% for men.

Among both men and women, the non-response can be ascribed in 7 out of 10 cases to a refusal to participate in the survey. Two out of ten cases of non-response are due to the fact that the persons selected could not be contacted, and in 1 in 10 cases an interview was impossible because of sickness, language difficulties or some other reason (Callens, 1995). Compared with other recent sample surveys, NEGO V occupies the middle ground.

The response rate for both men and women shows virtually no variation according to age. Differences do however exist according to civil status: non-response is highest among divorced persons, lowest among married persons (women: 39% and 28%; men: 44% and 32%). Non-response is also higher in urbanised municipalities.

NEGO V used a fieldwork method to compensate for non-response: stratified random substitution of non-respondents of the target sample (panel b) by persons selected from a reserve sample. The success of this method depends on two conditions: 1) random substitution and 2) a sufficient number of attempts to contact non-respondents. The interviewers were instructed and supervised accordingly. Substitutions were made at random, but not always after sufficient contact attempts. Non-response by persons in the target sample was not offset entirely adequately by substitution of these sample persons. Stratified replacement (cluster type) results in compensation for non-response, whereas random replacement (age, civil status) does not. There is no systematic compensation for the age and civil status variables (Callens, 1995). In the future, a multiple stratified substitution procedure could compensate for the non-response for different variables simultaneously.

A total of 2,897 women and 1,878 men were interviewed. How representative is the complete NEGO V sample (*Table B.1, e*)? In terms of age, there is an under-representation of younger persons. Married men are likewise under-represented.

The non-response rate in the survey in the Brussels Capital Region is higher than in the survey carried out in the Flemish Region (52% of Dutch-speaking women; 39% of Dutch-speaking men). Roughly one quarter of the persons in the target sample could not be contacted. There is no obvious link between non-response and the age of the person contacted. In this survey, too, the substitution method was used. A total of 339 women and 320 men were interviewed (Daelemans & Callens, 1994).

Table B.1 The survey population and non-response (NEGO V, Belgium/Flemish region)

Birth cohort	Women: Single	Women: Married	Women: Previously married	Men: Single	Men: Married	Men: Previously married
a. Number of eligible persons according to national statistics						
66-70	166,400	30,989	178	197,847	9,160	18
61-65	73,350	143,308	4,054	125,146	103,295	1,570
56-60	27,809	175,500	11,692	51,162	163,019	8,098
51-55	14,453	169,215	15,733	26,659	166,400	13,399
b. Number of persons in target sample						
66-70	462	231	1	378	70	1
61-65	186	595	29	213	309	11
56-60	79	649	47	77	416	32
51-55	45	595	56	54	393	35
c. Number of persons interviewed						
66-70	323	157	0	265	41	0
61-65	114	441	21	121	221	7
56-60	44	490	28	44	286	16
51-55	22	414	34	32	265	21
d. Percentage of target sample not interviewed[a]						
66-70	30.1	32.0	100.0	29.9	41.4	100.0
61-65	38.7	25.9	27.6	43.2	28.5	36.4
56-60	44.3	24.5	40.4	42.9	31.3	50.0
51-55	51.1	30.4	39.3	40.7	32.6	40.0
e. Number of persons interviewed after substitution (= total number interviewed)						
66-70	437	214	0	386	58	0
61-65	158	623	25	172	324	8
56-60	66	656	44	71	394	21
51-55	33	595	46	40	369	35

[a] Computed as 100*(b-c)/b.

7.3 The Dutch survey (OG'93)

The sample

The Dutch survey is a representative sample of men and women living in the Netherlands and born in the period 1950-1974 (i.e. around 18-42 years of age at interview), regardless of their marital status, country of birth or nationality. Of these 3.1 million men and 3.0 million women in the population on January 1st 1993, approximately 3,700 men and 4,500 women were interviewed in the period February to June 1993. A random sample was taken in two steps. In the first step, according to the number of addresses in proportion to the total number of addresses in the Netherlands, municipalities were drawn from the Geographical Basis Register. In the next step, the actual addresses were drawn. At each address, persons aged 18-42 years, up to a maximum of three, were invited for an interview.

Data Collection

The interviews of the NFFS'93 were held face-to-face by experienced interviewers from Statistics Netherlands. All interviewers were women, mostly middle-aged. During instruction meetings, the objectives of the survey and the potential interview problems were discussed. The interviewers pre-screened the addresses by telephone, so addresses where nobody in the 18-42 age range lived did not need to be visited. Since the first months of 1993 were peak times for Statistics Netherlands interviewers, logistic problems forced SN to pre-screen sample addresses by telephone for the presence of appropriate candidates (the method of pre-screening reduced the number of visits from around 30,000 to 10,000). The difference in response between addresses screened by telephone and those not screened only amounts some 0.5 percent. This means that the influence of pre-screening is small.

Laptop computers, now standard in Statistics Netherlands interview practice, were used for the first time in fertility and family surveys. The questionnaire was written in BLAISE, a computer language developed by Statistics Netherlands, which has the advantage of automatic routing and built-in controls to prevent inconsistent replies.

Response

The sample consisted of 19,998 addresses to be visited by interviewers during the first half of 1993, of which 1,103 could not, for various reasons (no time, illness, no dwelling unit) be contacted. The response from the remaining 18,895 addresses in OG'93 can be evaluated at address or household level, or at person level.

Response at address or household level

In 39.0 percent of the households contacted there was no respondent in the age bracket concerned. At addresses where someone was eligible for an interview, the response at household level (at least one person responding) was 48.5 percent. This response is in line with other recent SN household surveys. In general, in the Netherlands, public willingness to participate in surveys is lower than in most other countries. Explicit refusal accounted for 2/3 of the total non-response rate. In the end, 5,599 households were interviewed.

Each responding household could contain more than one candidate. In 3,191 households there were two eligible candidates. In only 17 of the 5,599 responding households were there more than three eligible candidates. In these households, only three candidates were selected. Response decreased with the number of eligible candidates. Of the 3,191 households with two candidates, 76.8 percent (2,450) of the households responded completely. In the cases with three candidates (132), only 47.0 percent (62) responded completely. Per household, on average, 1.57 respondents were interviewed.

Response at person level and selectivity in response

The 5,599 responding households resulted in 9,102 candidates, 90.3 percent of whom agreed to an interview. Some selectivity in the response became visible. Among other things, men participated less than women. Moreover, when a household consisted of more than one person, men and children participated to a lesser extent. Older men refused more often than younger men, while among women, the younger ones refused more often. One explanation for this result is that, among men, mainly the heads of households refused to respond (they are often older).

Weighting

Some of the characteristics of the responding population in the NFFS'93 could be compared with integral population statistics or with the results of other surveys. Based on these comparisons, the results were weighted at person level. The weighting procedure was carried out separately for men and women. Background variables in the weighting procedure were year of birth, marital status, household position, nationality, number of inhabitants per municipality and - only for women - the number of live-born children.

7.4 Note on the use of MCA

Multiple Classification Analysis (MCA) is used, i.e. a linear regression model with categories of variables coded as dummies. This technique is specifically appropriate in the case of nominal explanatory variables. Before evaluating the regression model, MCA computes the grand mean of the dependent variable and then gives, per category of the background variables, the deviation from this grand mean. Per category of each explanatory factor, both an unadjusted and an adjusted percentage are calculated. The adjusted values reflect the 'own' influence of every explanatory variable on effect. Where the term 'eta' is used in the tables, this shows for every explanatory factor what the (bivariate) correlation is with the dependent variable. The beta is the partial correlation coefficient, i.e. the correlation if other factors are adjusted for (i.e. kept 'constant'). The total explained variance shows which part of the differences in the dependent variable are explained by all explanatory factors together.

All background variables are displayed in the tables on each occasion, even if the effects are not significant in order to make the comparison between the two countries and different aspects of the dependent variable easier. For the dummies, however, only those that are significant are displayed in the tables. If, according to the MCA model, a specific independent variable is not significant (at a $p = 0.10$ level) 'n.s.' is placed above the adjusted deviations for that variable.

References

Callens, M. (1995), *De 'Fertility and Family Survey' in Vlaanderen (NEGO V, 1991). De gegevensverzameling*. Brussels, CBGS Document, 4.

Cliquet, R.L., F. Deven, M. Corijn, M. Callens, E. Lodewijckx (1992), *Conceptual and analytical Framework of the 1991 Fertility and Family Survey in Flanders (NEGO V)*. Brussels, CBGS Werkdocument 82.

Daelemans, I. and M. Callens (1994), *De "Fertility and Family Survey" in Brussel*. Brussels, CBGS Document 6.

Latten, J.J. and M. Widdershoven (1993), The 1993 Fertility and Family Survey. (pp. 75-79), In: *Netherlands Official Statistics. Population Statistics (Reprint 5)*. Voorburg: CBS.

Latten, J.J. and P.F. Cuyvers (eds.)(1994), *Relatie- en Gezinsvorming in de Jaren Negentig*. Voorburg: Centraal Bureau voor de Statistiek (Statistics Netherlands), Hoofdafdeling Bevolkingsstatistieken.

Latten, J.J. and A. de Graaf (1997), Fertility and Family Surveys in Countries of the ECE Region. *Standard Country Report. The Netherlands*. Geneva: UN/ECE Economic Studies No. 10c

Lodewijckx, E. (1999), Fertility and Family Surveys in Countries of the ECE Region. *Standard Country Report. Belgium*. Geneva: UN/ECE Economic Studies No. 10k.

European Studies of Population

1. J.-P. Gonnot, N. Keilman and C. Prinz: *Social Security, Household, and Family Dynamics in Ageing Societies.* 1995 ISBN 0-7923-3395-0
2. H. van den Brekel and F. Deven (eds.): *Population and Family in the Low Countries 1994.* Selected Current Issues. 1995 ISBN 0-7923-3396-9
3. R. Cliquet and C. Thienpont: *Population and Development.* A Message from the Cairo Conference. 1995 ISBN 0-7923-3763-8
4. H. van den Brekel and F. Deven (eds.): *Population and Family in the Low Countries 1995.* Selected Current Issues. 1996 ISBN 0-7923-3945-2
5. H.A. de Gans: *Population Forecasting 1895–1945.* The Transition to Modernity. 1999 ISBN 0-7923-5537-7
6. D. van de Kaa, H. Leridon, G. Gesano and M. Okólski (eds.): *European Populations: Unity in Diversity.* 1999 ISBN 0-7923-5838-4 (HB)
7. J. de Beer and L. van Wissen (eds.): *Europe: One Continent, Different Worlds.* Population Scenarios for the 21st Century. 1999 ISBN 0-7923-5840-6 (HB)
8. J. de Beer and F. Deven (eds.): *Diversity in Family Formation.* The 2nd Demographic Transition in Belgium and The Netherlands. 2000 ISBN 0-7923-6461-9

KLUWER ACADEMIC PUBLISHERS – DORDRECHT / BOSTON / LONDON